Under
— the —
Streetlights

Matt Deisen

WESTBOW
PRESS*
A DIVISION OF THOMAS NELSON
& ZONDERVAN

This book is a work of non-fiction. Unless otherwise noted, the author
and the publisher make no explicit guarantees as to the accuracy of
the information contained in this book and in some cases, names of
people and places have been altered to protect their privacy.

WestBow Press books may be ordered through booksellers or by contacting:

WestBow Press
A Division of Thomas Nelson & Zondervan
1663 Liberty Drive
Bloomington, IN 47403
www.westbowpress.com
1 (866) 928-1240

Because of the dynamic nature of the Internet, any web addresses or
links contained in this book may have changed since publication and may
no longer be valid. The views expressed in this work are solely those
of the author and do not necessarily reflect the views of the publisher,
and the publisher hereby disclaims any responsibility for them.

Any people depicted in stock imagery provided by Thinkstock are models,
and such images are being used for illustrative purposes only.
Certain stock imagery © Thinkstock.

ISBN: 978-1-5127-4409-5 (sc)
ISBN: 978-1-5127-4410-1 (hc)
ISBN: 978-1-5127-4408-8 (e)

Library of Congress Control Number: 2016908856

Print information available on the last page.

WestBow Press rev. date: 08/02/2016

Table of Contents

Dedication

To my wonderful family, for asking tough questions and encouraging me to do the same.

Foreword

I was standing with a friend in a forest in the mountains of California. It was a starry, moonless night. The midsummer air was warm and clean. Satellites visibly traversed the vast expanse of the domed firmament – the sky didn't have to compete with the city lights.

My friend and I were Christian high school students at a Christian youth retreat, singing worship songs to Jesus around a bonfire with hundreds of other students.

I asked my friend, "Do you ever wonder if any of this is real?" I surprised myself with my own question.

Pulling his eyes away from the sky, he asked, "If any of what is real?"

"Jesus. Christianity. The Bible. I'm a pastor's kid. I was raised in the church. I don't know any different," I said hesitantly. "I'm starting to wonder if it's all real. Do you ever *wonder*?"

At first my friend didn't say anything. Then he smiled, turned his gaze back to the stars, and said, "I like to wonder."

That was it. For the first time in my life I saw the twin cravings of wonder and doubt as just that. Cravings. Wonder is to reality as thirst is to water. It's like a magnetic field emanating outward from the heart of the Really Real. Wonder is when we feel the pull.

Doubt is just as vital as wonder. Doubt is to faith as hunger is to food. An unhealthy relationship with doubt can be deadly. On one hand, fear of doubt can lead to binge-eating on fetish fact claims and ultimately fundamentalism. On the other hand, love of doubt can lead to a kind of spiritual anorexia in which doubt and deconstruction themselves become codependent addictions. On that summer night under the stars, I paid my respects to wonder and doubt. Things haven't been perfect between us, but I'd like to think wonder, doubt, and I have shared a healthy relationship ever since.

My friend Matt Deisen felt the pull of wonder and doubt from the "other side." While my doubts contested my belief in God, Matt's doubts contested his belief in naturalism. My doubts carved a hole in my faith big enough to fit a universe. Matt's doubts exposed cracks in the edges of the universe through which he has come to know an even bigger God. This is why I find Matt's story so compelling. The same magnetic field of wonder that pulled me away from certitude also pulled Matt away from skepticism. Now Matt and I journey together toward the Really Real. Matt tells his provocative, personal story in this book, *Under the Streetlights.* This book is a friend's invitation to engage honestly with wonder and doubt, and to consider where those twin cravings are leading all of us.

In one of my favorite stories from the Bible, Jesus is standing with his friends in a clearing on a hilltop near Jerusalem, Israel. The Mediterranean air is crisp and dry. This wouldn't be such a big deal if Jesus hadn't just risen from the dead. Now he's standing in their midst. Alive. In

Matthew 28:17 we see the reaction of his disciples: "When they saw him they worshiped him, *but some doubted.*" Some doubted! The resurrected Jesus is now physically standing before them, and *some still doubt.* That is fascinating to me. It gets even better. In his very next statement, Jesus *still commissions* them all. To believers and doubters alike he says: "Go, and make disciples." On that hilltop alongside the risen Jesus, the believers and the doubters both belonged. On that mountain with my friend, I came to know that deep sense of belonging. In *Under the Streetlights,* Matt's story provokes us to open up to the best news in the universe: We are all invited to *belong* to something bigger and more beautiful than we dared to dream.

Evan Wickham

Introduction

My name is Matt. This is my journey from atheism to Jesus.

Truth be told, what you are about to read started as a letter that I wrote to a friend. I arrived home one night after a thought provoking and heartfelt conversation with one of my friends, and immediately began to put my thoughts on paper. Once I began writing I had trouble stopping, an unusual thing for someone who rarely writes. Having written far more than intended, I went back and broke my thoughts into chapters to make it more readable. Having accidently written a book, I believe that I have benefited as much from writing it as anyone might benefit from reading it. When we try to define what it is we believe, when we try to put it on paper, it changes us. Something transformative happens.

Now that it is finished I have nothing left to do but pass it on, and hope that what you are about to read will be beneficial, or at the very least thought provoking. I recognize that the words you are about to read are imperfect. All we can do is speak from our own experiences, and even those will be varied and limited. But by no means does this imply that we should keep quiet.

Dear *****,

In light of the many discussions that we've had, I felt a pressing need to continue our last conversation on paper, so that both you and I might have something to think over. Perhaps it is just a part of being young, but it seems we have spoken often about some of life's biggest questions, and because I am young I do not know that I can correctly answer them. While I admit to being inexperienced and perhaps unprepared to fully articulate the concepts that follow, I also believe that these things cannot go unspoken. Life is too short to keep quiet, and there are too many things I want to share with you before we become old and set in our ways. I pray that we will always be the type of people who ask tough questions and seek satisfying answers. May we never stop chasing down the mysteries of life.

In all my searching I have found only two constants in the world: change and God's love. I pray that we may learn to embrace them both with open arms.

1 Thumbtacks and Maps

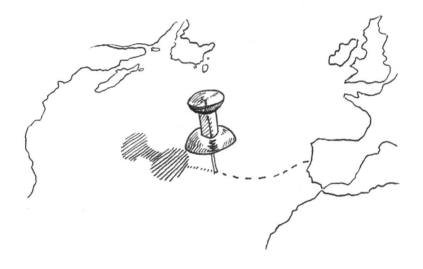

A life of total dedication to the truth also means a life of willingness to be personally challenged. The only way that we can be certain that our map of reality is valid is to expose it to the criticism and challenge of other map-makers.

– Dr. M. Scott Peck

When I was in fifth grade, our class did a project on the early European explorers. Our teacher pinned a giant world map to the wall and told us to pretend we were in the sixteenth century. She then gave us thumbtacks to use for ships. Each kid was assigned a crew of classmates, and we were each crowned with the flag of a different European country. With our thumbtack ships in hand, we could explore the world. We set out across the Atlantic and went wherever we wanted. It was our responsibility to stock up our ships, carefully plot our course, and scheme about which land we wanted to claim. Great challenges and danger were awaiting us as we embarked. Compared to algebra it felt like a real adventure second only to recess. The game was set up so that in order to move our ship, we had to answer trivia questions, turn in our homework on time, and throw away our trash in the proper bin. The thrill of crossing the Atlantic (in competition with our new adversaries) held our interest like nothing else. It was hands down the best school project I've ever had.

I used to imagine I was the captain of that ship, setting off across the Atlantic, charting new seas and braving unknown dangers. I faced the elements (and my enemies) with gusto and confidence, while my shipmates looked to me for courage. These are the things that capture a boy's attention.

I'm convinced every boy longs for adventure.[1] It is written into our hearts to seek out something epic. We long to raise the anchor, set sail, and aim our bows at the horizon. We long to charge into the unknown. We want to chart new lands and claim new territories. We long for that triumphant moment when a mysterious continent is spotted on the horizon. We long to find land that we've never seen before. We long to find land *no one* has ever seen before. Little boys want to be the ones who write new maps and make new discoveries, and if we can take the cutest girl in class along for the ride, then we are on top of the world.

My fifth-grade project was off to a good start. We must have been turning in our homework or throwing away our trash, because we were almost in the front of the pack in no time. Nobody had died of scurvy and things were looking up. We had the trade winds at our backs and were closing in on the front-runner when I had a startling realization. We were halfway across the Atlantic and about six nautical inches from discovering the unchartered land of America when it hit me, *there was no land left to be discovered.* We'd mapped out the whole world. We weren't discovering America! It had already been found—and then conquered, crossed, plowed, settled, plotted, and paved. I was sitting in the suburbs on the West Coast. America had been fully explored, every mile of it had been picked over. *All of it.* There was

---

[1]   Maybe every girl does too. But I'm not a girl, so I don't really know.

the globe, sitting right there on my teacher's desk, under the American flag next to the pencil sharpener. It was complete. By now, we had ten thousand satellites circling the earth taking pictures of it in case Columbus missed something.

The moment I had this epiphany the wheels of my fifth-grade mind started to spin and I was struck by a terrible thought, *"My life will be ordinary. No swords and castles. No masts and sails. No pirates and scurvy. Just classrooms and boardrooms and babies."* I would be stuck doing homework, commuting, and changing diapers for the rest of my life. People like Colu I cannot get mbus, Magellan, and Lewis and Clark had taken all the fun for themselves. We were left with nothing but Google Earth and plenty of time to think about how much fun they must have had when the world was an adventurous place. Back when life required courage and people didn't know what was over the next mountain range. Back when no one knew what waited for them on the other side of the ocean.

But where was that frontier now? Where were the unchartered territories for me to discover? I was having my first life crisis at the age of ten. I figured I had little choice but to resign to the ordinary. I figured maybe life really was all about exceeding in the classroom, so I could make it the boardroom, so that someday someone would want to make babies with me (at which point I would offer to change their diapers).

It wasn't until I got older that I realized we live in a world that is wild and full of adventure. It took years for me to realize the truth: *we are all mapmakers*, each and every one of us. Each one of us builds a map of his or her world. We form and shape what we believe about the nature of reality: scientifically, emotionally, and spiritually. We explore, ponder, and chart our discoveries as we travel through time, and there is much to be discovered. There is more to discover here than we might ever have time to chart, ponder, or understand. It is the struggle of discovery with all of its joys and pitfalls, the process of navigating our way through this reality, that *is* the very process and adventure we call life.

This journey, this process of building our map of reality, is not unlike real mapmaking. It is enlightening and painful, exciting and uncomfortable. There is great risk involved, and it requires great courage. Sometimes we have to do our homework in order to move the ship, but it's all worth it if we can discover new lands.

It is in the spirit of mapmaking that I have written this book, because I believe there is a desire buried in each one of us, no matter how neglected, to reach for new horizons, challenge our own assumptions, and brave new territory in the name of discovering the frontier we have been born into. Each of us hopes to one day grasp the beauty of the reality we live in, and without fanning the flame of this desire, we will never discover how deep and rich our lives can be.

May you never stop exploring.

2 Setting Sail

The first day of kindergarten is always an exciting day. Most parents coach their kids for the big day. They teach their kids why you shouldn't punch people, how to ride a bus without a legal guardian, why you should listen to your teacher, and why you should be nice to everyone. Most kids have to get psyched up for the first day of kindergarten and be encouraged along the way, because it's one of the scariest moments in a young kid's life. I remember my first day of kindergarten. The anticipation was palpable because I was about to do something without my parents.

I probably had new rain boots, a new backpack, and an unopened pack of crayons. I don't remember the details but what I remember clearly is walking into my first day of kindergarten and into a new world. My teacher showed us around the classroom, told us not to punch each other, and assured us we'd be able to ride the bus home without a legal guardian holding our hands. She then sat us down to tell us about all the exciting things we were going to do and learn in this new institution called school. I think she was trying to ease us into the fact that most of us were going to have our wild little spirits broken as we became enslaved by a system of gold stars, verbal warnings, and parent-teacher conferences. But I loved my kindergarten teacher and she made everything sound like a lot of fun. We were going to learn how to spell. We were going to create art. We were going to learn how to play chess. We were even going to learn about animals. *"For example,"* she asked, *"does anyone know why a flamingo's feathers are pink?"* My little hand shot up from the back. Don't ask me how I knew to raise my hand. Maybe they teach you that in preschool. *"Because they eat shrimp!"* I called out. Don't ask me how I knew the answer. The teacher was shocked. In twenty years of teaching no kid had ever gotten it right. It was the first and last time in my life that I was at the very top of my class. It was a great first day. I probably should have quit while I was ahead.

To this day, I don't know why I knew stuff like that. I think it's because I asked a lot of questions. I loved asking questions when I was a kid. I wanted to know everything. I wanted to know why a plane stays suspended in the air but a feather falls to the ground. I wanted to know why the sky was blue during the day but clear at night. I wanted to know why a candle goes out when you blow on it but a fire only gets bigger. I wanted to know how grass could grow. I was curious.

I liked asking questions. All sorts of questions: what, when, who, and how? But my favorite questions, hands down, were the "why" questions. "Why?" is a powerful question. It's the type of question that moves us. "Why" questions are active and dynamic and they capture our imagination. "Why" questions are the key to rethinking, reimagining, and reinventing the world around us.

Some people think "why" questions are a waste of time, a pointless distraction, but I think they propel us forward. They lift us off the couch and send us out into the world to discover new things. I think genuine questions act as the sails of the mind, harnessing the wind of our thoughts and thrusting us toward the horizon. An open and inquiring mind is a powerful force. In the world of map-making, it is the only prerequisite to genuine exploration.

Not only that, but I am convinced we are supposed to ask "why" questions because we are the only creatures on Earth that can. Other animals can ask basic questions.

My dog used to stare at me with her head tilted off to the side, and I am nearly certain she was trying to ask me something. We are not alone in our ability to ask basic questions, but our species has the exclusive ability to ask "why" questions, which implies that we should ask them often. They are a unique privilege that we get to exercise. I think something deep in our hearts was built to ask "why" questions, and because we are the only creatures on the planet that can, it would be terrible waste if we never did.

I am convinced that we were designed to ask tough questions, because there are powerful and landscape-altering truths out there beyond the horizon waiting to be found. Answers waiting for those who are bold enough to lose sight of their own shore in search of new places. They are waiting for the explorers and the adventurers, and just like the explorers of centuries past we need the courage to seek out the unknown beyond our horizon *and* the humility to redraw our maps as we go. Too often we make our map of reality based on the painfully small world in which we have confined ourselves. We accept the artificial limits we have imposed on ourselves, never bothering to look beyond the mountains, never risking what might be discovered if we ventured beyond our own shores.

The genuine mapmaking level of inquiry takes courage because we embark in the face a long list of fears, and the greatest among them is the fear of uncertainty. There is no guarantee that we will ever find answers to our "why" questions, let alone answers that are satisfying and true.

Perhaps you are afraid that you will start asking questions, only to find yourself tortured by a lack of answers. We fear being stranded in a vast sea of speculation, only to feel frustrated and lost. But if we are to discover the deeper truths of our reality we must place a higher value on truth than comfort. No one ever discovered something worth finding from the comfort of the couch.

As a middle class American, I fear that we have overcommitted to our couches and idolized our own comfort, and in doing so we have confined ourselves to the ordinary and the mundane. But the problem is that no child's heart dreams of the mundane. We were designed for something far greater. There is something in us that was meant to be awakened, something deep and spiritual and true. There is a part of our hearts that is slowly numbed by the ruts of routine, demanding work weeks, an onslaught of daily advertisements, and the consuming self-indulgence into which life so often seems to slip.

Asking questions is about being awake. Inquiry awakens us to the possibilities and potential that exist around us. It opens our minds to see a picture of reality that is bigger than us, and sends us searching for those things which most desire to be found. The opportunities we have at our fingertips are staggering in their importance, and if we are mentally, emotionally, and spiritually sleeping we will miss out on them completely. It is a great trick of the devil that we should be lulled to sleep as we go through life; drifting aimlessly and without purpose, never grabbing hold of the reigns, never questioning the state of our reality or where it's all headed.

You were designed for more than a numb and fleeting life. You were designed to ask tough questions, and (in seeking their answers) you were meant to encounter something true about the world, something true about yourself, and something true about love and the nature of our universe. You were designed to be awake and flourishing in a way that most of us can hardly grasp or understand, and without genuine inquiry we will never enter the life we were designed to experience. I've written these words with the hope that you will encounter such a rich and meaningful life.

3 Life

Life; \'līf\ (noun):

1. The buzz of electric energy that flows through atoms and molecules, giving consciousness to things that have consciousness, and awareness to things which have awareness.
2. A collection of otherwise lifeless materials from which something greater emerges and dwells.
3. A sequence of collective experiences that distinguishes us from rocks.
4. The seventy year nine-to-five grind that we experience between birth and death.
5. The strangest occurrence in the material universe.

When I was young my family went on a lot of adventures. We didn't have much money, but we were intentional about getting off the couch and doing things. I grew up in Washington outside of Seattle, and there were loads of opportunities for camping, hiking, and exploring.

When the Northwest started to feel too small, we would take road trips, loading up the family vehicle with big bags, big dogs, and big plans. It was a great way to grow up. We saw most of the country at one point or another, and when we had finished a long day of hiking in the Sonora desert, snowshoeing on Mt. Rainer, or camping in the Everglades, my mom would gather her three kids together and always ask the same question. She would look back from the front of the car, or the other side of the tent, or across the aisle of an airplane and ask, "Who feels lucky?!" and the three of us kids would respond in unison "I do!"; and we knew that we were.

I no longer think of my life in terms of being lucky or unlucky anymore, just blessed. Whether you know it or not, you are blessed too. The mere fact that you are reading this says a lot about you. It means that your genes survived thousands upon thousands of years of disease, famine, predation, and war. Of the dizzying number of possible genetic combinations that could have been created by your parents, you were the one. You ate food today, you can read, and you are alive, which means you are very blessed.

You and I have been given the rare and incomprehensible gift of life. We have the chance to feel sorrow and fulfillment, victory and defeat, the opportunity to fail and succeed, to love and to hate, to create and to destroy. You can make choices, make friends, make enemies, and make babies. You have the opportunity to conquer, exploit, observe, love, heal, and restore the world around you and the world within you. Our planet is bursting with beauty, from the distant polar ice caps to tropical deep-sea vents, and everything in between, but I am convinced the most complex and beautiful organism on this extraordinary planet of ours is a human being. Human beings are remarkable creatures—remarkable to the point that we might actually be considered a miracle.

There are many people who say they do not believe in miracles, but I believe the very minds from which those thoughts emerged are themselves miraculous. It is almost beyond my comprehension that you and I started as tiny specs, smaller than a pinhead. You started as a microscopic combination of DNA strands; almost nothing, yet containing so much.

You were once a little spec, but inside that spec was a mysterious energy. Inside that spec was a sort of knowledge, a plan, a creative force that defies the imagination, and I would argue there was *intention*. We typically think of a miracle as once-in-a-thousand-year event. Most people lump the concept of a "miracle" in with fancy magic tricks and spectacular anomalies: when the natural laws of our universe are bent or broken, when probabilities are beaten, or the unexpected occurs at the moment we need it most. We equate "miracle" with walking on water, healing the blind, the conquering of terminal cancer, or the melting of an impossibly hard heart. These are miracles, but so are you.

You and I are essentially the dust and minerals of old stars—with one key difference. We have this strange energy pulsing through us, this thing called life that we often forget is flowing through our veins and animating otherwise lifeless particles of dirt. You are made of billions of cells that can collectively contemplate their own existence—a physical body, and so much more than a body.

Have you ever stopped and pondered how strange it is to live and breathe and have *consciousness*? Have you ever stopped to wonder why we have five fingers and five toes and we're stuck on a tiny rock in the middle of an endless universe that stretches out in every direction? Have you ever thought about what our universe would be like with no life at all? What if there was not so much as a mosquito to observe or experience the entire material cosmos? What if consciousness did not exist? Have you ever wondered what it would be like if it was all just dust and air and gas and black holes swirling around and around each other, without the sound of a song bird to grace the air, or a mind to marvel at what has been made? I have. I think the universe makes more sense without life. Life is impossible. I honestly cannot decide sometimes which is more bizarre: a material universe without any conscious life to observe it, or conscious life itself.

Sometimes I am simply amazed that my chest continues to rise and fall, or that my body can take frosted mini-wheats and turn them into new skin cells for that scrape on my knee. I am amazed by the fact that I have a mind that can contemplate, experience, ponder, and *know* things. When a spec of *anything* can grow into everything that we are the word miracle comes to mind. It defies logic. Life is amazing. We are more complex and unexpected than we typically give ourselves credit for. You are a body animated by life, complete with a heart and soul (the depth of which we still cannot comprehend) and these incredible and illogical things beg that terrifying question that every mapmaker needs to wrestle with.

Why?

4 Amoebas of the World Unite

For most of life I lived in the Seattle area, but in 2010 I moved down to Portland, Oregon to start law school. Up to that point I had never owned a car, but I heard that everyone in Portland rode their bikes to work, so the week before I moved down I bought my first road bike from a guy on craigslist for a hundred dollars. The guy had four bikes in his little apartment, which seemed suspicious to me, but I was overjoyed to get my first real road bike. The bike itself is orange and silver with handlebars that are set awkwardly low and gears that don't shift right. The bike does not even have a brand name on it. Years later I still have cyclists in Portland who ask me what type of bike I ride and I still have no idea. I just say, "It's orange." The mechanics at my local bike shop told me that I could probably find them at Wal-Mart, which is doubly insulting in Portland. It was far from perfect. But what did I care? The moment I purchased it I had my mast and sails, and I was ready to see the world.

A week after buying the bike I packed up everything I owned and trucked it down to Portland. I arrived a week before classes started, but I wasn't in the mood to start studying yet. I knew the first year of law school was going to be brutal, so I decided my first week as an Oregonian would be better spent getting to know my new state than buying my text books and sitting in the law library. After all, I would have three years to live inside thick books and I was in no rush to get an early start.

I suddenly found myself with a new road bike and a week to kill, and there was only one logical adventure that came to mind: bike the entire Oregon coast. I called up my friend Jake and pitched the idea to him. We would start in Washington, bike the entire coast of Oregon, and end in the Redwoods in California—camping along the way. It was a flawless plan, except that neither of us had ever ridden a road bike before, we didn't have the right equipment, and we had no idea what we were doing. Jake immediately said yes. He didn't even own a bike yet. I could not ask for a better friend.

I am a dreamer, and the best thing dreamers can have around them are people who say yes a lot. It's no good for a dreamer to have friends that criticize and over-analyze and give you 101 reasons why your idea won't work. A dreamer needs friends who will just say yes and jump on board. It takes a certain personality to say yes to an invitation like the one I posed to Jake. Not many people would agree to bike 400 miles when they don't own a bike.

Jake and I packed up my mom's SUV and headed for the coast, stopping on our way out of town to buy Jake a bike. He spent a whole fifteen minutes in the bike shop and came out with a new road bike and a bag full of new gear. We loaded everything up and headed west toward the Oregon coast and Highway 101.

For those who haven't seen it, Highway 101 is one of the best highways on the planet, and I'm not just saying that because I live on the West Coast. I have traveled most of America and half the world and I still think the 101 takes the cake for greatest highway. It is hard to compete with a thousand miles of rugged coastline, dramatic cliffs, giant sand dunes, mile long beaches, and old growth forests. It has California wineries, picturesque coastal towns, the Columbia River, San Francisco, the Olympic Mountains, the Redwoods, Big Sur, and Los Angeles; how do you compete with that?

After driving for an hour and half Jake and I reached the coast, mounted our new bikes, and turned south. I stood at the edge of the Pacific with my used road bike. Nothing but the pure potential offered by 400 miles of coastline lay in front of us. It felt like standing on the deck of a wooden ship with a charter from the Queen of Spain to cross the Atlantic. We set our sights down the coastline, and started peddling. Here, finally, was a real adventure. The kind that little boys long for—and this one was not made of thumbtacks and paper maps. It was real, and we felt the rush of exploration as we set sail.

As the miles started to roll by our legs began to ache and burn, having been rudely awakened from their apathy. Jake and I had not trained for this. We had not done so much as a practice ride. It's hard to train if you don't own a bike. At least that was our excuse. But the funny thing about excuses is that they don't stop your legs from burning.

The first day was the hardest, but what we lacked in training we made up for with sheer excitement and determination. It is amazing what your body will do when you refuse to let it quit, and the 101 was beautiful enough to distract us from the pain. After awhile it starts to pull you along, and within no time the miles started to drift by. Around each corner was another breathtaking view, beckoning us down the coast. The Pacific is rugged and wild, and you would be hard pressed to find a better place to bike. The 101 follows the coast, sometimes lazily winding through coastal towns and along flat beaches, other times forcing us to cling to the side of cliffs overhanging the ocean. More than once a semi-truck rumbled by, sending a rush of air over our shoulders as we prayed that our bike tires would stay on the road, all the while looking cautiously down at the ocean as it rolled and foamed hundreds of feet below.

The threat of death, however vague, always makes you feel a little more alive. You don't get that enough in the suburbs. I think there is something in the heart of a man (and maybe all people) that comes to life when everything is on the line—when we feel that rush of danger and uncertainty. I think part of us is at war with our suburbs and cities, with our business meetings and grinding commutes, because deep down we long for the frontier. Some part of us longs to face death and brave the wild places. We were made for more than excel spreadsheets and favorable employee reviews.

During the week we biked the Oregon coast, the 101 was our wild place, and it displayed the Pacific in all of its West Coast glory. Oregon beaches are rugged and untamed, and for the majority of the year you need a sweatshirt to really enjoy them. Storms roll in over the ocean, pounding the coastline with rain most months of the year. Not many people fly to Oregon for her beaches, but for those who thirst for something wild and untamed, these are the best beaches in the world.

Jake and I continued on our adventure, and the days started to drift by as the coastline slowly unraveled before us. That week was the most time I had ever spent on the coast, and being near the ocean changes you. There is something timeless about the Pacific. It is full of energy and life, yet it stands unchanged through the millennia, and when you sit at the edge of it, it almost invites you into that timeless space.

I like the ocean because it feels both ancient and new at the same time. It has to be one of the oldest things on planet Earth, yet it makes you feel alive. The Pacific Ocean is particularly endearing because in Oregon we get to sit on the beach and watch the sunset. There is nothing quite like a sunset over the Pacific—especially when you have a mile long beach all to yourself. Luckily we have a lot of wild beaches in Oregon, and Jake and I had caught our fair share of good sunsets that week.

As the days started rolling by, we slowly but surely made our way down the coast. There is nothing quite like experiencing a coastline on your bike. It makes you feel uniquely connected to the place, and there is something strangely gratifying about having to earn every inch. I will never forget the rush of salty sea air constantly blowing off the ocean. I will never forget cruising through sleepy coastal towns, camping night after night on the beach, and catching glimpses of orca whales as they patrolled the coastline for food.

Dozens of sleepy towns dot the rugged coastline, and old growth forests come spilling down the coastal range, colliding with the sand and surf. The fog seems to constantly roll off the ocean, turning to drops of dew that cling to the trees, as waves crash endlessly up onto the beach, and humpback whales glide lazily up and down the coast, shooting mist skyward out of lungs the size of a car. I was completely enchanted by it.

By the sixth day we had cycled over three hundred miles and into Southern Oregon, and we set out to tackle a rugged stretch of coastline. A strong headwind slowed our advance—burdening the miles that slowly unfolded as our calves pushed and burned. By mid-afternoon we had finally reached our destination. Despite taking a ten-mile detour to visit an old lighthouse, it was our earliest finish of the week and we unexpectedly found ourselves with time to relax. We arrived and set up tents at our little campsite, and Jake and I, who had been inseparable up to that point, went our separate ways. Jake went to hunt down a shower, and I wandered out to the beach to soak in the scenery.

The Southern Oregon coast is captivating. Islands dot the horizon, providing safe harbor for the seals that gather on them, as seagulls call to each other, suspended motionless on the ocean breeze. Taking a deep breath, I could taste the saltiness of the ocean as it entered my lungs. All I could hear were crashing waves and a lazy wind. The distant hum of a truck engine drifted into earshot and back out again, somewhere off in the distance, gliding along the 101. The next day we would hit the California border and then the Redwoods; we had almost made it.

There was a sense of stillness and peace out there, on those rugged and hidden beaches. Towering stone monoliths lift up out of the sea, old and defiant, standing strong—despite the fact that the land around them abandoned its post long ago. They look like majestic stone towers, or the crumbling columns of some ageless and mythical city—as if they were the ruins of some ancient civilization that was lost to the sands of time. They have an air of royalty about them.

As the hours drifted by I watched as the sun sank lower in the sky setting the clouds ablaze with orange and red. Jake and I had seen some good sunsets in the last six days, but this was the type that takes your breath away and pulls you in so deep that nothing else in the world exists but you and the ocean and that brilliant ball of light, as if the Kingdom of Heaven itself was waiting there, just over the horizon. The sun danced off giant waves as they came rolling in from some distant land, traveling over the deep places of the ocean, before finally crashing into those defiant monoliths and continuing their relentless march to the shore.

The Pacific Ocean is one of my favorite places on earth. It captivates me because it is unknown and mysterious. We know more about deep space than the deepest parts of the ocean. The mystery of it sends shivers down my spine. The ocean pulls us in because even though aspects of it are mysterious, parts of it are also accessible and freely available to us. There is something powerful about sitting at the edge of the ocean. When you sit there and stare out at those endless waves, you cannot help but be impacted by it. There is a mystery and a peace surrounding it. It feels like home.

Some people think that we came from the ocean. They think that all of life started with little cells and amoebas swimming around out there. According to the theory, which I like to call "amoeba theory," little bits of life were floating around out there in the ocean. Little cells came into being that were alive, and these little cells learned how to make copies of themselves, and they kept copying themselves and growing and changing until more complex and better cells were made. It just kept on like that for a long time, until finally, after enough time had passed, humanity was born. At least that is what we learned in school. It used to make sense to me.

But standing at the edge of the Pacific, watching the sun bounce and dance off the incoming waves, I was struck by the absurdity of it all: that little amoebas could come crawling up out of the ocean to laugh, dance, sing, write poetry, and love each other. I tried to picture it in my head—little amoebas moving through the ocean like miniature jellyfish, a billion years ago, slowly bumping into each other and deciding to be friends, and then recruiting more friends to join their cause.

I try to imagine the little amoebas joining together to form bigger and better things until they formed a human being. Something about it is so strikingly odd, the idea that a series of random events would lead to such a profound result. When I try to break it down in my head, I can only picture amoeba theory happening two different ways.

First, I imagine that the idea for humanity was hidden deep inside the first little cells that came into being. The potential for the human project was concealed somewhere in the depths of those first little cells, just lying in wait until the right time to emerge. Those cells were like seeds, full of potential, pregnant with humanity.

Now I'm not the smartest guy around, but the only other way I can picture it in my mind is that the potential for humanity was somehow waiting out there in the universe. The only alternative I can imagine is that the idea of "human" existed outside of our little amoeba friends, and they stumbled across it. Almost as if the idea was an oversized set of clothes, waiting for our amoeba friends to grow old enough to put them on. As if we were out there, in the realm of theory and hypothetical possibilities, waiting to be invited onto the dance floor of creation.

I guess a third alternative might say that some cosmic force could have suggested the idea to them, or hid the idea out there in the field of potential that exists in our universe for our amoeba friends to stumble upon. But I don't think amoeba theory easily allows for "cosmic forces" intelligent enough to suggest such an idea.

Confused by the alternatives, I attempted to reduce it to math, like an equation:

amoebas + time + pressure = humanity

But it didn't add up in my head. That equation didn't compute, so when math failed I tried art. Perhaps each of those first little cells were like a distinct color on an canvas, and some artist combined them in brilliant arrays and combinations. This instantly sounded more plausible, but the art theory would beg for a Sculptor or Cosmic Artist, and amoeba theory does not allow for those conclusions.

These are the things I think about on vacation.

As the waves crashed and the seagulls flew overhead, I stared out at the waves and wondered what on earth could have set this all in motion. I tried to picture our little amoeba friends building on one another until they became something completely unexpected—like fully functioning eyes, contracting muscles, and brain cells that could imagine new possibilities, think thoughts, and dream dreams. The whole thing teeters between surreal and impossible. We tend to take this whole "life" thing for granted, but I don't think we should. I cannot really wrap my head around amoeba theory any more, but even if amoeba theory were true, it would make you question things. You would have to wonder what sent our little friends climbing up out of the ocean to write symphonies and brew beer and land on the moon. The whole thing borders on the impossible. Life is just too bizarre.

As the sun burned into a deep red and started sinking into the ocean, I was overcome by a sense of joy and purpose. In that moment it was overwhelmingly evident to me that life is an unexpected occurrence. It begs for an instigator. Life is screaming for a source. It is the type of phenomenon that requires inspiration. Life defies logic and intuition.

I am convinced that any reality that starts as nothing and arrives here is so spectacular that there *has* to be more at work here than most of us are prepared to admit. The simple fact that photosynthesis happens in plants, in the middle of a nearly lifeless universe, begs for a reason and subtly demands an explanation. It whispers of a source far beyond itself.

We accept reality because we are here and we cannot easily deny our own existence. We try to rationalize it based on rock samples, fossil records, and "logical theories" that allow for an existence that is likewise straightforward and rational—perhaps even one that requires no contribution from things we cannot see. But I am no longer able to look at the Pacific Ocean, or the Redwoods, or humpback whales and say with a straight face that we all got here on accident. There is something intentional about life, something so beautiful that it escapes words, and there is something unique and distinct happening in you and me.

I have tried to picture all the uniqueness of who we are emerging from the ocean. I tried to picture this thing called "love" emerging from a sea of random chance and lifeless atoms, but I can't connect the dots in my head. There are many people who are much smarter than I am, so it is perfectly possible that I am just not smart enough to grasp it all, but for some reason I cannot conceptualize hope being born out of a petri dish. I cannot visualize morality, justice, or the capacity to dream emerging unprovoked from a primordial soup. I can't get on board with the idea that our capacity to love owes its existence to the growth and propagation of single-celled organisms, or that we stumbled into these capacities in the desperate scramble to increase our chances of survival.

Amoeba theory would say that our souls were the result of lifeless molecules bumping into each other over time. Which would require us to believe that compassion, mercy, and kindness were born in a vacuum. It implies that the concept of God is nothing more than a cheap Band-Aid that people use to cover up the woundedness of an empty existence, and that your sole purpose in this life is to consume resources, reproduce, and die. Amoeba theory posits that our minds, hearts, souls are the result of an unbalanced equation in a chaotic universe governed and ruled by "random."

But it has become increasingly difficult to believe that we came to be without rhyme or reason, without source or inspiration. I think in order to believe these things I would have to close the eyes of my heart as well as my mind. I think there is more going on than meets the eye. A divine conspiracy is unfolding around us, and if we close our eyes to it, we risk missing the very reason we are here.

5 The God of Blank Spots

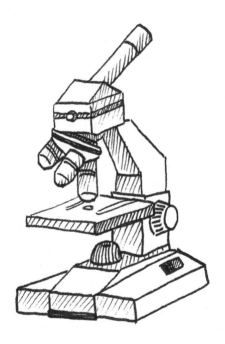

When I was a kid I loved science. In fact, I still do. I first fell in love with science in the third grade. My third grade science teacher was named Mr. A. He was really passionate about the scientific method, conducting experiments, and centrifugal force, and as a result I was taken in by it. It turns out passion is contagious. When we see someone who really loves something, they bring it life. They make it lovable. That is what Mr. A did for science, and I never looked back.

I loved anything that had to do with science, especially the elementary school science fair. All my classmates would come together and make volcanoes out of vinegar and baking soda, or do tricks with magnets and electricity. One of my friends had his dad help him build a hovercraft, powered by an industrial vacuum. It was awesome. I loved every minute of it, and it hardly mattered whether it was the science fair, science class, or just reading books about science, my little brain ate it up.

Science captured my imagination because it is a whole field of study devoted to searching for truth. It is an entire discipline focused on finding hidden realities that are out there for us to discover. It is all about diving under the surface and pushing past the superficial in order to uncover bits of truth buried in everything from our psyches to our solar system. Science, at heart, is really about exploring the frontier—and the more we discover on that frontier, the better we are able to thrive in the world.

Science is what gave us car engines, washing machines, iPhones, automatic razors, cures for polio, and images of deep space. Science offered my young mind a chance to explore the frontier, to set sail and sink my teeth into something true. It gave me permission to ask questions—big questions—and then set out to find their answers. Science was a chance to explore unchartered territory and find things that no one had ever discovered before.

At the heart of science is the scientific method, which is a means of analyzing the world that is focused and objective. It encourages us to ask questions, but it also encourages us to be skeptical of our answers. We were taught to accept what is provable, observable, and repeatable, and as a result this became my worldview.

I was raised to be an "open minded skeptic." I think it was part of the culture I grew up in. The scientific mindset spilled over its disciplinary boundaries and carried well beyond the walls of Mr. A's classroom. The culture I grew up in was in some sense a scientific one. On the one hand, I was raised to be open minded about the world, its people, and the things those people believed, but at the same time there was not much room for believing in things that were not proven and repeatable. I was skeptical to the core. I did not believe in anything I could not see under a microscope. If something could not be published in a scientific journal, it probably wasn't true. Believing in the unproven things, in the unseen things, in the "faith things," was at best illogical and at worst downright dangerous.

As a result, people who had faith did not make sense to me—at least the ones who had faith in God. I guess we all have faith in something. Scientists have faith in their methods and their worldview, and back in the day when I believed in amoeba theory (and a godless universe) those views required faith as well. But that is a different kind of faith. Faith in the scientific method and worldview hardly felt like faith at all, but faith in God was a strange animal. That type of faith was foreign, unfamiliar, and uncomfortable. The very concept of God seemed naïve and archaic, and therefore a blind faith in Him seemed incredibly dangerous.

I thought that God was an outdated substitute for science. I figured that we invented the idea of God because we did not understand the world around us. I assumed that throughout history, as humans observed their universe, we naturally had a lot of question marks and were confused about how things worked. There were a lot of "blank spots" and gaps in human understanding, and too many unchartered continents on our life maps.

So I figured that someone way back in ancient history must have said, "*You see all these gaps and questions marks? They are all part of this thing called 'God'.*" At which point (I assumed) those ancient people took the idea, and (in their ignorance) ran with it. In other words, faith was based on superstition and misunderstanding. Back in the day, people did not understand how babies were conceived, what a solar eclipse was, or what made people sick. I figured we just said it was "God" because we did not know any better. I thought God was a figment of our ancient imagination. It is easy to believe in our skepticism.

God was simply an invention of the human mind that was used to fill in the question marks and to satisfy our own curiosity. I thought it was our fear of the unknown that drove us to invent a higher being.[2] But as science was marching forward, it exposed the truth; it was really

---

[2] Let's be honest, most of the things that we invent out of fear of the unknown are not good things at all. It was fear of the unknown that drove us to invent ordinary, and ordinary is boring.

gravity, microbes, genetics, solar eclipses, or disease—not God. Now that we understand static charges and plate tectonics, we have no need for Zeus or Atlas.

It seemed as if "God" was really just a God of blank spots and "He" (or "it") was shrinking as our gaps in understanding were filled in by science and logical thinking. In my view, science was the marvel of our modern age—an amazing field of discovery and truth—and as it marched forward it was shedding light on all the maddening superstitions that were clinging to us like the foul residue of some confused and ancient culture. Humanity's lingering belief in God was just a hangover from the dark ages when people had faith because they didn't know any better.

So when it came time for me to draw my map of reality and decide what I believed, I had to ask myself that sacred question, *"Matthew, how do you think we got here?"* The answer (for me) was an easy one. I had not really considered God in the equation at all. The random play of molecules in a lifeless universe gave birth to us, and that was simple and sound enough for me. I was not aware of any legitimate school of thought that challenged the notion of "random chance," and I was quite comfortable believing it. The only group that really seemed to make any attempt at discrediting amoeba theory was the Church, and I did not take them as a serious threat. They were all faith and no logic; they were all bark and no bite; they were all legend and no truth. They were scared of science and I loved it, and they seemed to simply discard anything that would threaten their doctrine. At least that is what I believed in my skepticism, back when science was my worldview (and in a sense my god). But it was not meant to last.

Eventually I was confronted with a new landscape that forced me into the uncomfortable work of redrawing my map. Eventually I was confronted with something bigger than fantasy or legend—something as real as any scientific discovery could be—something that flipped my world upside down. All of sudden everything changed. Well not everything. I still find the creation debate fairly interesting, because science is still my favorite subject, but now that ancient, provocative thing called "God" has become the center of my life, and the Scriptures have a lot to say about God and the role He played in creation.

The Bible records a fascinating account of how the universe was created—and I would venture to say it is often misunderstood by people on both sides of the creation debate. For the longest time I did not understand it. I mean, I still don't fully understand it, but that is not for lack of trying. The first sentence of the Scriptures says, *"In the beginning, God created the heavens and earth."*[3] It may be the most important sentence in the entire Bible, because if you believe that God does in fact exist, and that He created the universe, then everything else in the Scriptures is a piece of cake. If that first sentence were true, it would mean we live in a world without limits; that anything is possible for the Creator who fashioned it. It would mean that everything else contained in the Scriptures is not only plausible, but perhaps even highly likely. If you believe that there is an all-powerful Creator, then nothing else in the rest of the Bible should really shock us, aside from the depth of His love and the genius of His plan.

---

[3]   Genesis 1:1, New International Version.

The problem is most of the people in my city don't believe God exists, and they certainly don't believe God created the world, and therefore everything that follows that verse is cast into doubt. For most of my life I didn't believe it either, and as a result nothing in the Scriptures made much sense. I was caught in the crossfire between amoeba theory and the creation account. I was stuck in that tension.

Even today, there are questions and tension. I approach the subject with a lot of humility, knowing that I don't really know much. But then again, some of our most brilliant thinkers and theologians can't seem to figure it out either. When it comes to the Scriptures, biblical scholars cannot agree on how to best translate the Hebrew writings into English, or even how to interpret the English sentences after they have been translated. Is this a poem or is it literal? Is it scientific, figurative, or artistic? What would Genesis have meant to the people it was originally written to? What should it mean to us?

There are dozens of seemingly legitimate theories concerning what Genesis is and what it tells us. Biblical estimates of the timeline for the creation of the world range anywhere from seven days to untold billions of years. Some scholars think the Scriptures are describing the creation of the entire universe (from start to finish) in seven days. Others think that billions of years may have passed before God used seven days to create and set aside a small patch of earth known as the Garden of Eden. I think the biblical theories are right. Not because they all agree (because they don't). But I think they are right because they place God at the scene of the crime. They agree that He was the instigator, that He was there at the kick off, that He orchestrated life and set in motion the very reality we are experiencing.

The biblical account says simply and emphatically that God is not a "gap filler," footnote, side note, or scientific question mark, but rather that God is a real Being that created the universe. God is the Source with a capital S. But there is something else that I find striking about the creation account in the Scriptures. The building of most of the material universe, and the potentially vast period of time that accompanied it, takes up as little as a single sentence in the Bible (or several pages at most, depending on the interpretation you subscribe to).

My Bible is approximately twelve hundred pages long. It maps out the human heart and the human story with startling clarity. It tells the story of a God who knows me better than I know myself, a God who is just getting started with our universe. I have come to believe that it is true and reliable. But it's not a textbook; it's not a scientific journal. It does not say a word about how molecules came into physical existence—back when there was no such thing as a molecule. I bet physicists would have loved that. It does not say anything about dinosaurs, despite the fact that archeologists (and most six year olds) would have loved that. It does not say anything about the distant reaches of our universe, how the sun keeps burning, or what black holes are all about. Astronomers would have loved that. But God did not reveal those things to us.

I am convinced that the Scriptures are primarily meant to capture God's interaction with humanity, and that anything that occurred before the moment the first human took their first breath is ultimately a tantalizing mystery that is neither central to our faith or necessary for understanding God's future.

The Scriptures offer us an unparalleled look into the human heart, and more importantly, into the heart of God. The Scriptures give us the chance to comprehend our reality (and the God who created us) at a depth that would be impossible in their absence. The Bible reveals to us that we are actually living God's story, and it gives us powerful glimpses of where everything is headed. It gives us a backstage pass to the human experience, to the "why" behind sin, struggle, work, service, laughter, joy, love and death. The human experience itself is defined, explained, and put in context—and creation is an important part of that context. It is central to our experience. Birds and trees, mountains and star fields, friction and gravity all matter to us, and the Scriptures tell us they were born out of God's inventive power. In other words, He set the stage. He designed the universe, He made it possible, He set it in motion, and when it comes to understanding the cosmos, or more importantly *our place in the cosmos*, the bottom-line uncompromising takeaway from the Scriptures is this: *God created it*. That's the message. That's the big idea. The Bible is not meant to explain genetics, or medicine, or how far away the sun is. It is not meant to explain plate tectonics or how creatures adapt to their environments over time. It did not give us airplanes, or microwaves, or the Internet—that is not its purpose.

The Scriptures claim that God orchestrated the kick off, that He launched the whole project—and if that were true, it would change everything. It would mean that we were created with intention, whether it took seven seconds or seven billion years. It would mean that life is full of intrigue and wonder, that a tantalizing mystery is unfolding all around us. It would mean that we have the chance to invite that mystery in close, so close that it would unfold inside of us, in the deep places of our hearts that we cannot fully understand. It would mean that our lives are infused with purpose, direction, and meaning. It would mean that you were born into a world of unbounded possibilities, and that the limits we place on our own hearts and souls would be pointless lies and unnecessary restrictions.

If the bottom line takeaway of the creation account were true it would open the door for all sorts of possibilities . . . even eternal life. When I read the brief account of creation, I walk away thinking one thing, *"This place is amazing, it once was nothing, and God created it."* God made life possible; He created you; it's personal. The creation account lays the foundation for understanding life from a human perspective. The Bible is a divine proclamation of sorts—one devoted to the human story, to humanity's place in God's universe, and to humanity's future in God's Kingdom. That is the whole point.

I am not here to advocate for one interpretation of Genesis over another—you will have to decide that for yourself. You may hate those first pages or you may love them, but either way you have to wrestle with them. Personally, I like the first few pages of Scripture because they tell us that God made us and that we are here by His will and intention. It allows us to see that our lives are rich with purpose, and we are not simply little cosmic accidents afloat on a rock in a vast and empty universe, whose purpose is to experience lots of pleasure impulses on the gray matter between our ears before we meet our inevitable and final end.

God starts His announcement by saying, in essence, *"I am your Founder and your Creator. I am not even just a powerful Being who stumbled upon this world, but I made it possible, I crafted it, I am its Author. It is the object of my love and affection, and I am big enough to redeem it. I knit you together in the womb, and you may call me Father."*

6 Wonder and Awe

W hen I was little my two favorite holidays were Easter and Christmas. They were awesome. Like most Americans, I didn't grasp what they were about, or why they should change my life. Nonetheless, they were the two best days of the year, and in some sense they did change my life because I was allowed to have all the candy I could eat.

Every family tends to develop holiday traditions that are special to them. Ours were Pop-Tarts. We were not allowed to have Pop-Tarts during the regular part of the year, but two days a year (Christmas and Easter) we would go all out. As Easter approached we would buy boxes of Pop-Tarts in eager anticipation—the day of gluttony would soon be upon us. The night before Easter, the three kids would drag our sleeping bags into my parents' room to sleep on their floor. We would all lie in our makeshift beds and attempt to fall asleep in spite of our excitement. I'm sure you know how difficult it can be to fall asleep on these special nights, but of course we all knew that if we were unable fall asleep then the Easter Bunny wouldn't come. Duh.

There is always a bit of mystery (and skepticism) surrounding the Easter Bunny when you are a kid. It is a tough call for parents. Our parents let us believe there was an Easter Bunny for a while, and I think at first I actually believed them. How else could all those amazing little chocolates get put all over our house while we were sleeping in a circle around the foot of my parents' bed? Our dog wasn't smart enough to do that. It must have been the bunny![4]

---

[4]   Bunny was (ironically enough) the name of our dog.

41

In any case, the three of us would wake up Easter morning and head out into the hallway, where a special curtain was always hanging, blocking our view of the glory that awaited us in the rest of the house. The curtain always hung from a shower rod stretched across the hall, and I will always remember the white with blue and red polka dots. We called it the "smiley guy curtain," and our little eyes nearly burned through it in anticipation of what was on the other side. For the life of me, I cannot remember why it was called the smiley guy curtain, but you rarely question those things as a kid. What I do remember is that we would line up in order of youngest to oldest (youngest in the front of course) and then wait for our parents to give us the signal. They would talk to us from the other side of the curtain as they surveyed the house like forward scouts, informing us that the Easter Bunny had in fact come, which I think was supposed to mean that we had been good little kids, but I am not really sure.[5] In either case, our little eyes would nearly burn a hole in the curtain as we waited for our parents to say the magic word, and then we would burst through the smiley guy curtain and out into the glory. Our house had been transformed. It was filled with wonder and awe and . . . chocolate. Our excitement was uncontainable.

The three of us would go nuts, scrambling from place to place and searching every nook and cranny. My mind was blown by the fact that there were tasty chocolates hidden

---

[5]   I guess it could have meant that somewhere, someone had made an adequate sacrifice on the Easter Bunny Alter, which I can only assume would be located somewhere in Scotland because Scotland is the only place that sounds magical enough to have bunnies that lay eggs.

all over our otherwise ordinary home. Those little eatable mysteries brought new life and intrigue to every square inch of it. Every piece of furniture became important, every picture frame had potential, and windowsills became downright exhilarating. Our entire house was alive with the potential for discovery, which is what made Easter the best. There was nothing else quite like it.

My parents were wonderful to do that year in and year out—to hide things for us to discover. It just would not have been the same if we had casually walked out Easter morning to find our prepackaged and pre-assigned baskets with our names on them. I mean, chocolate is still chocolate, but the holiday would not have been the same. Something about my parents' willingness to hide chocolate created an atmosphere of discovery and excitement.

It was not until I grew older that I started to wonder if God might have done the same thing. I wonder if God has hidden endless mysteries in our universe so that we can discover them, like some sort of cosmic Easter egg hunt. I think maybe He buried mysteries in our DNA, deep space, and beneath the earth's surface so that we might search for them and find them. Not only because there is a senseless complexity in their beauty and depth, but also because something in our hearts loves the mystery and we long to hunt it down. We love surprises. That is why we wrap gifts in paper, and play hide-and-go-seek. That is why, year after year, my parents would buy Pop-Tarts, hang the smiley guy curtain, and wake up at some ungodly hour, just to dazzle us. There is something in us that longs to seek and discover. We love to explore the frontier. That is why Americans crossed the Atlantic in wooden ships, then crossed the Great Plains in wooden wagons, and then set our sights on the moon. We love surprises, we love adventure, we love the frontier—and God was good enough to give us one.

There was something enthralling about searching for those little chocolates and discovering them. If our Easter tradition had been to quietly sit down and open a bag of prepackaged chocolate—calmly eating what we wanted in an orderly fashion—something would have been missing. Don't get me wrong, it still would be awesome: chocolate is still chocolate, and we would still be kids. But we would be missing out on something deeper. We would be missing out on the wonder, awe, and sheer joy of seeking and finding, of searching and receiving. We don't get nearly enough of that type of joy in our lives. Halloween falls short of it, let alone Presidents Day. That is why Easter captured our little imaginations and sent chills of delight down our spines.

The Scriptures say that God delights in concealing things, and I think our scientists, doctors, mathematicians, and elementary school students delight in discovering them. Which is a beautiful thing because our universe is designed for discovery. Between the depths of the ocean, the far reaches of space, and the complexity of the human heart, we have endless frontiers.

Most people believe there is a grinding tension between faith and science, and many of us feel torn by it. Some people fear that if they accept God, they will have to turn their backs on science and logic. Others think that if they listen to science and nod their head in agreement then they will have to turn their backs on God. Neither is true. But at some point early on, perhaps in my adolescence, it seemed as though following God and believing science directly opposed each other, and that accepting both simultaneously would significantly diminish what either one had to offer.

Ultimately, however, I realized God is not the opposite of science. He is the *reason* for science. He is the reason why a speck of DNA grows into a human being and a tiny seedling becomes a towering red wood. He is the power behind life itself. God is the Creator and Designer of the entire universe; He is the founder of everything that we hope to gain a deeper understanding of through science. Nature is His art, and His inventions range from the laws of physics to the subconscious mind. The consciousness that stares through your eyes was a gift from Him. Life was breathed into the soil and the sky and sea by God's will. He set the stage of our reality, the same reality that scientific study hopes to observe and explain.

Science is still one of my favorite disciplines. It has the power to reduce a seemingly chaotic world to charts and graphs, and from that information we can find cures for our diseases, build airplanes, and understand more about the circulatory system, but the best parts of life can never be converted into measurements or explained by science, and it would be a shameful thing to wish that they could.

Science makes for a great discipline, a lousy life philosophy, and a downright awful religion. I think when I was younger I abused science by making it my belief system and the basis of my entire worldview. I inadvertently joined many others in our culture by idolizing science and asking it to play a bigger role in my life than it was ever intended to play.

Science is comforting because we naturally value certainty, repetition, and predictability. Science gives us a sense of comfort and security, it helps us control and understand our world, and its precepts are certain, repeatable, and predictable. Faith is none of those things. God may give you comfort and security beyond anything this world can possible provide for you, but faith does not grow in the land of certainty. God's Spirit cannot be seen, His movements are not readily repeatable, and God Himself is not predictable. He is not easily measured or understood—but neither is love, or the perfect song, or the beauty of a sunrise. If we only believe in what is certain, repeatable, and predictable then we will miss out on the very best that life has to offer.

For some people faith feels logical, God is apparent, and His faithfulness feels as certain as any scientific principle, but faith itself will never be factual. Faith will never be math, and if it were it wouldn't speak to our hearts. If faith could be reduced to charts and graphs there would not be much left to enjoy, and it would not capture our imaginations and ignite our hope. That is why we simply cannot allow science to be the primary language of our hearts—because all of the most important things in life lie outside of the scientific realm: beauty and God, love and justice, wonder and awe. Therefore if science is all we know, then we will either miss or misunderstand the heart of what it means to be human.

If science and math are the only languages our hearts know how to speak, we risk taking too much for granted. We tend to lose our sense of wonder about things that science has labeled or in some sense explained. For example, a thousand years ago we did not know much about how babies were made, but now we know that two sets of DNA are actually combining to form a human being at the molecular level. We can watch the fetus grow through every stage. Perhaps we can even predict what color eyes the baby will have and what diseases they might be susceptible to. We understand a lot more about the process. But does that make the creation and birth of a human being any less of a miracle? Does the fact that we can watch a tiny spec grow into a living, breathing, moving, thinking, loving creature make it any less shocking? I don't think so. We know more now than we did then. It has become more known and therefore less *mysterious*, but no less *miraculous*.

Astronomy tells us that the stars are a vast distance from the earth. So far, in fact, that some of the stars could have gone out millions of years ago and we would still see their light in the sky. That's cool. I love learning crazy facts about our universe, and measurements are great, but I also think we were meant to go lay out in grassy fields on warm nights and look up at the stars in wonder. I think it is plausible that those endless galaxies were strewn about the universe to dazzle us. Perhaps they were born out of God's uncontainable majesty. Perhaps God's glory longed for self-expression. Perhaps there is a song of grace and wonder written into that starry night sky. Perhaps there is a deep mystery embedded in it that was meant to tug at our hearts.

People of faith sometimes feel threatened by science, but I think the only threat that the scientific worldview poses to faith is that if we only measure things objectively we may forget to experience them in our hearts, *and we need both*. It is a pretty bold and outlandish claim that God may have spread out the material universe to dazzle us in an act of bold self-expression, but what if it were true?

What if by some crazy miracle that was reality? It would be a shame to get to the end of everything and know how far away the stars are, what trajectory and force you need to escape Earth's gravity, and what you would weigh on Neptune, without ever wondering at the beauty of it all and the God who made it.

We were meant to stand in awe of deep space, and wonder at the fact that it all started as a tiny pinpoint in space and time, only to explode outward in a radical act of creation. We were meant to ponder the sheer genius of DNA, the uniting force of life, full of creative power and brilliant design—as well as the Artist behind it. He is the mathematician that calculated gravity. He is the Architect who constructed the world in just such a way that we would have seasons, stability, and weather patterns. He invented rain cycles and unleashed them to create the Amazon and the Grand Canyon. He designed air particles in just such a way that they would be small enough to cling to the earth as it flies sixty two thousand miles an hour around the Sun, while remaining thick enough to keep birds suspended in flight. He created the Sun, Moon, and Earth and put them into a beautifully balanced dance; one that sustains life, keeps time, powers photosynthesis, creates rhythms of work and rest, and dazzles us along the way. You were meant to look up and be in awe.

I believe there is a deeper truth to our universe, and that science alone can tell us *how* molecules interact or *how* the neurons fire in the gray matter in our skulls, but it cannot tell us *why* the material universe is here or *why* it was so brilliantly crafted or *why* we have been given the ability to question our own existence. And in the total absence of the *why,* the *how* is ultimately empty and meaningless. It is only charts and graphs, only things we can measure, and the most important things in life simply cannot be measured.

We cannot measure God. Science has been unable to find God. Give me a team of the world's best scientists, put us a room with unlimited equipment and all the money in the world at our disposal, and we probably could not prove God exists. But go out into the world and you can see God at work. Search the depths of your heart and you might feel the gravity of God's presence gently pulling on it. God is real, and He is moving, loving, and redeeming. It is happening right now, and if wonder and awe are not emotions we know how to feel, it will be difficult for us to relate to the concept of God and perhaps harder still to freely worship Him. In order to seek, know, fear, love, and approach God we need some sense of wonder. This serves as the foundation for healthy worship. Wonder helps usher us into His presence and fuels our relationship with God. Wonder *is* worship.

When we come face to face with something as big and beautiful as God, the only fitting response is to stand in awe. I fell in love with God because He is incomprehensibly wonderful, and in that sense God is not unlike the Pacific. He captivates me because He is big and mysterious—too big for me to wrap my head around. We know more about deep space than the depth of His incomprehensible Being. He is mysterious and unknown, and yet part of God is accessible and totally available to us—at least to those who explore. But we are invited to come and sit at the edge and soak in the beauty of it, until it sends shivers down our spines. It's like sitting at the edge of the Pacific with the sun on your skin, just basking in the enormity of what lies in front of you. The more I feel out the contours of this mystery, the more I am struck by the sheer wonder of it.

I will be the first to admit that faith and science are different. Faith is about a real God working in the human heart. You just cannot bottle it up, package it, or put an equation to it. If our hearts only speak math, God will be confusing. The facts simply won't add up. The reality of God will not compute. And in the absence of total understanding we are left with two choices: we can ignore the concept of God altogether, blinding ourselves to that which does not compute, or we can simply stand in awe. I get the sense we were meant to do the latter.

Sometimes I wonder if this is what Jesus was hinting at when He said we should become like children. Perhaps we really should be like children, not in intellect of course, but in *spirit*. Children are good at experiencing awe. They are less resistant to being in a state of wonder. We need to be more like that. We need to have free and loving hearts that are not afraid to soar to those great and wonderful places. This is the ultimate evolution of the human spirit, because it requires greater spiritual maturity to stand in reverence, awe, and wonder than it does to take God, or our perceived absence of God, for granted. We miss this when our hearts are all charts, graphs, and skepticism. A healthy and curious skepticism can be good in the right context, but honestly sometimes we need to be skeptical of our own skepticism.

You were born into a world full of mystery, wonder, and divine romance. God is whispering your name and pursuing your heart. When we become aware of this reality, things start to happen. The world begins to change. You were born into a world full of grace, where unexpected things happen every day. We are invited to abandon our skepticism and live in awe—to embrace that wonder. You might think that accepting such an invitation is naïve, but what if it were the other way around? What if turning down that invitation only worked to blind us to the depth and beauty of the reality that we live in?

The beauty written into the code of your DNA begs for an intelligent source, and the Scriptures say that this Source has a name and your DNA bears His fingerprints. If it were true, we would need to rethink the world we live in. The implications are staggering. It would mean that you have a purpose, and purpose changes everything. In fact, I think the reason we are so passionate about debating our origins is that it speaks to our purpose. If our origins had nothing to do with our purpose, we would hardly debate it at all. Our origin creates the foundation of our identity, so when we sit down to contemplate our place in the universe we start by wrestling with our beginnings, because every theory of origin has implications of purpose.

One of the problems with amoeba theory is that it labels humanity as an accident. It says that we have a rather fleeting and inconsequential role in the universe, which (ironically enough) places each individual at the center of his or her own universe. The implications are clear. If humanity were an accident, it would mean that comfort, pleasure, and happiness would be the goals of human existence, and life would be all about the blind pursuit of these sensations. Pleasure and happiness would be sensations worthy of pursuing directly and for their own sake, regardless of the consequences. Anything that failed to give us those sensations would need to be avoided at all costs, and we would be armed with fantastic justifications for compromising of our own moral integrity and violating those around us. We could do it all in the name of our own pleasure and comfort. We might even become a people who say, *"This short life is all I have, so let's see what I can milk from it before I'm gone. This story is about me and my pleasure, screw everyone else."* If the world were an accident, it would fuel our self-centeredness. It would be the cornerstone of a narcissistic existence.

Even if you attempted to rise above self-centeredness and claim a larger, more altruistic reason for your existence, you would still be faced with all sorts of problems. For example, you could pretend that your purpose is not simply to protect the individual life that you find yourself directing, but rather to make sure that humans do not die out for a very long time. You could assume that the goal of "accidental humanity" is to steward the world in such a way that our species would be able to propagate and carry on for as long as possible. This thinking would allow for a much more stable and less selfish society. Suddenly it would be about *us* and not just about you. Life would involve protecting the planet (and one another) for the sake of our species. This theory would potentially curb any extreme self-centered and self-destructive behavior. This new collective purpose would meet the deep desire of the atheist to show reverence for life. It would even allow for the introduction of love, respect, and moral values as tools intended to help us get along. We could embrace all of it in the name of stability, reproduction, and the continuation of our species, while simultaneously avoiding that sticky topic called "God."

But even if you assume our purpose is simply to preserve the ultimate survival of our species, then our good or bad actions would still only matter to the extent that they affected anyone else's capacity to make babies and pass on their genes. That would still be a sad and empty world to live in. The individual life could still be very self-centered and pleasure seeking, even self-destructive, you would simply be asked to limit your destructiveness to your own life so that others could continue to seek pleasure and have the opportunity to make babies and continue the species.

We would still be left with no *true* purpose, no lasting hope, and no compelling truth to live for. The goal would be to make babies and die without hurting other people. This too is a stunted, sad, and ultimately empty way to approach life. No matter which way you approach it, viewing humanity as an accident has major implications when it comes to our identity, priorities, and morality. Purpose shapes the way we relate to our neighbors, our spouses, and the planet, and viewing your life as an accident directly affects your thought life, dreams, addictions, life goals, and sense of hope. If we are an accident, and you are the center of your own universe, then we have all sorts of problems.

The biblical account of creation, on the other hand, identifies humanity not as an accident, but as the purpose-filled pinnacle of creation. We are created, by design, with intention, and therefore we have a compelling reason to exist. The biblical perspective puts humanity at a more central and important place in the universe, while simultaneously *doing the exact opposite to the individual*. We are the crowning jewel of His creation. The crescendo.

The climax. We are made in His image. Humanity has a central role and purpose in God's story and the "why" behind creation. We are integral to understanding where this is all going. Yet as an individual, you were not built to worship yourself. You were not intended to occupy that central place of honor in your own heart.

The biblical account of creation challenges the individual to remove themselves from the throne of their own lives. It confronts the idea that we are the center of our own little universe of thoughts and actions. Our biblical purpose is actually higher than just food, sex, family, and getting ahead. Your biblical purpose may involve or include those things in a secondary or tangential way, and many of them are good in their proper context, but the reason that life is animating our bodies is far more profound than the routine of the everyday. It is more compelling than eating good food or even great sex. Our purpose is higher and grander than most of us have assumed. Some deep part of us is capable of embracing eternity. Our true purpose is divine, and that purpose is inescapably wrapped up in love.

7 Love

Love; *noun* \ˈləv\

1. That unspoken affection you have for family members or people who dress like you.
2. The magnetic pull of sexual desire toward an individual, occasionally accompanied by feelings of tenderness or a bouquet of flowers.
3. A strong feeling of admiration, fan fare, or friendship which you might feel toward a good friend, a (recently elected) politician, or your favorite super hero.

"Dear friends, let us love one another, for love comes from God. Everyone who loves has been born of God and knows God. Whoever does not love does not know God, because God is love."

– 1 John 4:7-8

Our capacity to love is the most important one that we possess. Ironically, "love" is one of the most undervalued and limited words in the English language. We really only have two words to express affection toward objects or people—"like" and "love." We typically have to choose between the two. So if someone asks me if I like Taco Bell I say "No man! I *love* it!" Or if my roommate offers to do the dishes after dinner I respond, "Yeah, I'd love that!" Anything beyond "like" falls into this generic blanket word that we call "love." Yet the way you love cheap tacos or desire a night away from the dishes is not the same as the affection you have for your parents, your friends, a significant other, or even a good book.

56

Other languages seem to have done a far better job at capturing the diversity of concepts embedded in the word "love." For example, in Greek there were several different words for love, all with distinct meanings. They had words like eros, storge, philia, and agape, each with related but unique meanings and uses. Different aspects of love were captured with different words.

I wish we had more words for love in English. I don't like using the same word to express affection toward my family as I do for a cheeseburger. It would be nice to have more than one overburdened little word, because I believe love is central to human existence. We need more words to capture its depth and variety, because collectively we should be able to speak more intelligently about something so profound. Love is so fundamental to our existence that it may be the very reason our lungs rise and fall. In fact, if we are to take the creation account literally and credit God with the creation of everything, then claiming that love is central to our purpose may be more plausible (and less ridiculous) then it first sounds. But to fully grasp this idea of love as purpose, we need to recapture the concept of love being a choice.

In America we mostly see love as a feeling. When people evoke a warm fuzzy emotion in us, we assign value to them for evoking those emotions, and the more warmth they evoke, the more value we assign them, and therefore the more we "love" them. Anything that gives us those fuzzy little electric feelings gets lumped into our over-burdened word called "love," and this type of love is only a feeling, but it is the strongest of feelings. It is this warm fuzzy feeling we call "love" that our culture lifts up as the exclusive justification and pre-requisite for marriage,[6] and we will do almost anything to find. It is so strong that people will spend their entire lives searching for it. We will fight and die for that feeling.

This electric love is fun and worthy of pursuit, but when we talk about love as something that is central and necessary to living a life that is abundant and full, we are talking about more than affection and electricity: we are talking about choice.

Most of life revolves around our choices. In fact, one could argue that the only two things we absolutely must do in this life are make choices and die. Choice is fundamental. When we survey the landscape of our choices and the options available to us in this vast universe, it becomes clear that the greatest of all is our choice to either love or not love. Just as fundamentally important is our choice to accept or reject love. Love is meant to be one of the most central and elemental ingredients of life, but it is also a word that needs to be unpacked. Love as a lifestyle is not the same as being in love, making love, or loving fast food.

The love that we really need is that type that you choose. It is the self-sacrificing commitment to love another unconditionally. It is divine love. That is the choice we have before us, and it is our choices that shape who we are. Love is an effortful and often difficult choice to make, and perhaps it is the difficultly of this choice and not simply its result that makes divine love the most meaningful act we can choose as conscious beings.

---

[6]   Consequently, society considers love's absence sole and sufficient grounds for divorce, because after all we *deserve* love, right?

Not only is love a choice, but *love is impossible without choice.* In the absence of free will you cannot love. I believe that this goes to the very heart of why we were given free will in the first place: because love is wrapped up in our purpose and we require free will to engage in it.

The Bible says that God *is* love. I think that is confusing to people who speak English. I think we lose track of God in the sinkhole of that overused word. We end up thinking God is simply the concept of affection or some positive energy that we feel when we are with the people we "love." We might forget that God is an independent Being. We might forget that our understanding of God was meant to inform us of what love actually is, not the other way around. Yet, because God is unseen and sometimes difficult to grasp, the reverse can also be true: a rich and full definition of love may help inform our understanding of what God is like in the first place.

A man named Paul wrote a letter to a young church in the first century. Despite all our modern day technology, education, brainpower, and enlightenment, it still takes the cake for the most inspired and accurate account of what love is. In his letter, Paul first explains that love is necessary if we are going to do anything worthwhile. He says that if we speak without love in our hearts we are really just a crashing symbol, adding white noise to the universe—it doesn't even matter what we're saying. Some of us were told growing up, *"If you don't have anything nice to say, don't say anything at all."* I think Paul is saying, *"If you aren't speaking in love, why speak at all?"* He says that if we know every hidden secret, crack every code, memorize every textbook, and have all the knowledge in the world, but we do not love, we have nothing. All of our wealth added no true value to our lives and all of our knowledge got us nowhere. You can even do the right things and give to charity and pay your taxes and be moral and enhance your species' chances of survival, but if you do it without love you have not advanced an inch.

This is the backdrop for explaining what love is. By now Paul's audience is on the edge of their seats. We understand that we might have oxygen, food, sex, safety, family, and respect, but we still may have missed out what it truly means to live. We might have climbed Maslow's hierarchy of needs, but now we sit at the top realizing that without love we have gone nowhere—the gain we perceived earned us nothing that truly lasts. Paul says that only three things will last forever: faith, hope, and love—and the greatest of these is love. What is this love that Paul speaks of?

"Love is patient, love is kind. It does not envy, it does not boast, it is not proud. It does not dishonor others, it is not self-seeking, it is not easily angered, it keeps no record of wrongs. Love does not delight in evil but rejoices with the truth. It always protects, always trusts, always hopes, always perseveres. Love never fails."[7]

You've probably heard this passage read aloud at weddings. Sometimes the newlyweds will even promise to be these things for each other. "I promise to be patient and kind and forgiving . . ." The promise is beautiful, but I have always questioned it. I can try really hard to embody Paul's words of love on my own steam but I never get very

---

[7]   1 Corinthians 13:4-7.

far. It is not the type of love that you can fake for very long. When I got married I promised my wife I would continue to pursue God in our marriage, because that made more sense to me. That is a choice that results in love, because when our hearts collide with His heart there is chemical reaction that occurs, somewhere deep down in our souls, and the result of that reaction is that divine love wells up in us.

God claims to be the Source of love, and He says we should focus on loving Him and drawing near to Him. When we do, His Spirit operates in and through us, and we are freed up to love others out of the overflow. He claims that He *is* love, and that we are the object of His unfailing love and unending affection. That means that God has lots of warm fuzzy electric feelings for us *and* He chooses to love us with an unconditional and sacrificial love. The combination of the two is insane, and when we catch wind of it we risk being changed forever.

8 Two Roads Diverged

When I was in the second grade our class had to memorize a poem by Robert Frost. The poem was sad and somber—even for a second grader. In the poem, the main character is hiking through the woods and he arrives at a fork in the trial where is forced to ponder which path to take. The traveler has to decide whether he will take the well-worn trail or take the road less traveled, all the while knowing that he will likely never return to this place again. The poem was full of longing and nostalgia, which are strange emotions for a second grader to experience. I am sure it was the oddity of these emotions that caused me to remember the poem after all these years.

Second grade was a good year. We had a giant stuffed dog named Balto that we got to check out and bring home with us. We got to watch live salmon hatch from their eggs in the classroom fish tank, but for some reason the thing I remember most was the poem. By the time I graduated elementary school, it was one of the few things I carried with me. I can still recite most of it two decades later.

The poem captures the struggle of a man who stands at a fork in his forest trail, contemplating which path to take. Staring down each road as far as he can see, he ponders which has the better claim. He has a sense in his heart that he will never return to this place, that the road he rejects will never be traveled at all. With a longing ache he chooses one of the paths and years later he reflects back and reminisces on his choice. He knows that he chose the road less traveled and that has made all the difference.

I think the poem struck me back then because it evoked some sense that there was a deep mystery to life and that

I had a choice whether to pursue it or not. I think it was sad because I realized that my choices would affect my life. No matter which road I took through the forest I was going to miss out on something. It was sobering because I realized that I had that control, that the choice lay in my lap, and if I took the wrong path I would not really be able to blame my parents, society, my DNA, or my second grade teacher. The split in the road lay at my feet. The choice was mine alone.

We have a lot of good hiking trails in the Northwest. To this day when I am out hiking and see a fork in the trial, I often hear that poem gently echoing in the back of my mind and I still try to take the one that looks less traveled. But the poem truly resonated in my heart because it is about more than just hiking trails. The poem is about something deeper.

Many years later—when I first starting reading the Scriptures—I was really struck by Jesus and how He talked about there being two different paths for us to follow. He claimed that we were standing at a fork in the road and that we had a choice to make—a choice that seemed to involve the human heart and mind in a holistic way. One path is narrow and the other is wide. One path is common and the other less traveled. One path is characterized by courage, the other by compromise. One path is selfless, and the other is . . . something less.

I do not understand many of the things Jesus talked about. Which probably puts me in the same boat as His disciples, because they followed Him around and learned from Him and lived with Him and they still didn't understand most of what was happening. All they could piece together was that Jesus was the real deal. I feel like that most days.

I'm not sure what Jesus really meant when He talked about the two paths, but I think the wide and easy path is just the default worldview of our culture. It is the traditional path of humanity, the one where we operate apart from divine love, or more specifically, apart from God. This is the path where we are primarily motivated by wealth, security, comfort, and reputation. Unknowingly, they enslave us as we walk, which basically is a dramatic way of saying that those desires control us. Those desires, those ends, govern us and color our minds. They inform us of what is right and wrong, what is wise and foolish, what is worth our time and what is not, *who* is worth our time and who is not. When we walk this path, we tend to care more about ourselves than anyone else around us. Not because we are evil or ill willed, but because we don't really have a compelling alternative.

Many people take that road.

But Jesus offers us a different path—a road that is less traveled. A path where we walk in the way of Love. The road less traveled is characterized not by its ease, but by its freedom. This road is characterized by light; it is the path where we walk in what God has for us, where we seek the will of our Creator. On the wide path we unknowingly tried to be our own god. On the road less traveled, we walk with the God who came for us. Jesus walked the path backwards, just so He could be there at the fork, to direct us. He came from a heavenly place down to this place so that He could be there to personally invite us down the road less traveled.

The fascinating and confusing thing about this path is that Jesus claims to *be* that path. He claims to *be* the Way.

One of the profound claims of the Scriptures is that God (who *is* love) became a human being—that He humanized himself. They claim that Love became a person. Which means that we can follow and walk with the embodiment and Source of love. We can communicate with Him and commune with Him and get wrapped up in that mystery.

Few people ever find that road.

This fork in the road that Jesus describes[8] between competing paths is actually a matter of what we choose to *worship*. Most people who don't go to church probably assume "worship" is something you do in a church. Most church-goers assume worship has something to do with music, but I think worship is actually much broader. Worship is all about giving your time, money, energy, and esteem to something, and if you will allow me to define worship with such broad strokes, the implication is that everyone worships something. We all give time, money, esteem, love, and respect to *something*.

The real issue, then, is that most of us do not pause long enough to really consider what it is we worship, and what we worship determines which path we walk. It becomes so central to our identity that it begins to color every aspect of our existence. There is something (perhaps something that only you know about) that you have placed on the throne of your heart. There is something you have dedicated your life to pursuing—the thing you want most, the thing you thirst after and hold high in your mind. That hidden thing that sits enthroned on your heart, the one

---

8   See Matthew 7:13-14.

that gets the bulk of our time, energy, and thoughts is the thing that you worship.

What we worship controls us. It guides us and informs us—so much so that the Scriptures say we are enslaved to the thing we worship[9] and more often than not, our slavery is rooted in fear. If we fear being alone we will worship family, significant others, and reputation. If we fear being vulnerable we will worship our wealth, homes, mutual funds, airbags, and home-security systems. If we fear being unloved then we will worship relationships, sex, or the praise and acceptance of others. We will go insane trying to make people love and respect us, even if it means we have to work the wrong job so that we can buy the right cars and wear the right clothes. Slowly our lives can become one vain attempt to eradicate all of our fears, and all the while we are enslaved to something that will never set us free.

When I was in high school, I had a pretty good life—I had a loving family and great friends, I was getting excellent grades and doing well in sports, I did not use drugs or drink alcohol, and I was well liked and generally happy. But I was a slave to the world and I worshipped my reputation, and the interesting thing about being enslaved to the world is that you don't see any chains or shackles. Enslaved people can put on a great smile, they can succeed, and they can get by just fine—that is why they continue to sit in slavery.

I used to dream about being wealthy when I was in high school. I wanted to marry a model, live in an oversized house, and drive amazing cars—hopefully at least two

---

[9] See Romans 6:16.

or three really amazing cars. I used to shop for my future sports cars online and think about which one I would buy first. The one I settled on was beautiful. It was going to look gorgeous in front of my nice house with my hot wife in the passenger seat. It could go zero to sixty faster than Google could load pictures of it, and it cost a mere five hundred thousand dollars. But I was also going to be a big shot lawyer, so the price wasn't going to stand in my way.

These were the dreams that constantly played through my mind and occupied my free time. They became an idol for me. I began to worship these dreams and live for them. Few people claim to be religious, but all of us are. Your religion is what you think about in your free time. Wealth was mine.

It was not until years later that I figured out the truth: the things I was worshipping do not satisfy. If I had achieved all the material wealth and status that I had drooled over in high school, I would have been sorely disappointed when I arrived because all of the things we worship on the wide path have something in common: they over-promise and under-deliver. There is nothing wrong with working hard to gain money, but when money takes a seat on the throne of our hearts we become slaves to money and that *is* wrong.

It is wrong because it is living a lie. It is wrong because it is unnatural. It is sinful because it steals your joy and you rip yourself off. You will delay your happiness, contentment, and satisfaction for the day that you finally achieve those "wide-path" dreams, only to arrive and find that you have a nasty taste in your mouth. We work so hard to seize the things we worship, only to find that there is still something missing and there is still a void—there is still an itch deep down in our hearts that drives us crazy.

Joy does not come standard with the next car, game system, or smart phone. Contentment is not delivered to your doorstep the day you become a homeowner, land that dream job, or get married. If the only happiness we know is the fleeting excitement of worldly achievements and possessions, then we risk wasting our lives on a fraud. The wide path is fun and engaging, and it is full of people to share the journey with, but it is so consuming that sometimes we forget how unnatural, unsatisfying, and crowded it is. We tend to accept the worldview of our culture without questioning it, and most of us swallowed the pill we were given. We have been reading off the script we were handed for so long that we hardly even recognize the foulness of the air we breath.

Sometimes I am disheartened by the fact that we are a nation so centered on television, but I guess what discourages me most is the quality of what we broadcast. The road most traveled claims most of our airtime.

By this point I am probably starting to sound like a religious nut, but I cannot help but be surprised and a little embarrassed when I watch some of our popular TV shows. The subliminal messages are there, and most of the time they are not even subtle. In most of our movies and TV shows the self-centered lifestyle is glorified and celebrated. The wide path is always taken, and it often ends with "happily every after." No STDs, single parents, unloved children, or post-success depression. There is no nagging sense of emptiness or genuine soul-searching, and so much of it feels fake. I cannot help but question how many of the characters from modern TV shows would actually experience genuine joy. It is disturbing that I come from a generation that grew up wanting to emulate a bunch of television characters who have pretty terrible lives. They have poor life philosophies, self-destructive habits, bad theology, cynical attitudes, a distorted sense of self, and (not surprisingly) no lasting hope. The result is what feels like the blind following the blind. We follow after the stars of Hollywood and evening sit-coms—a procession of self-glorifying, yet sadly empty people. Perhaps I over-exaggerate. I sincerely hope that is the case. But one of the most striking features of the road most traveled is that we honor and emulate people who never got it right to begin with.

As a result, the longer we walk the wide path the more harmful we become. We harm ourselves. We hurt our friends and family. We degrade and destroy genuine community. We leave less room in our hearts for love, true identity, and true purpose. We slowly stop caring about consequences outside of our own little bubble, mostly because we cannot afford to. We stop caring about the planet, we stop caring about the poor, and we stop caring about purity, justice, or righteousness—and right in the middle of it all *we are not satisfied*. The wide path is paved with gold but it only dishes out despair. The further we walk, the more hollowed out we become. There is a name for that. It's called hell. Right here, right now. We can live in that if we want to. The choice is ours alone.

The wide path is bursting with the mediocrity of self-centeredness, and the frustration of fruitless chases. Many people take that path, and Jesus reminds us that it is in fact *easy*. It may not be fun, it is ultimately unfulfilling, and it hollows us out over time, but it is still easy. You will not have to go against the grain; you will not be called out or set apart or challenged. You will never be asked to repent, humble yourself, or pursue righteousness, and you will always be surrounded by people who approve and encourage your choices, in secret hopes that your time on the wide path will justify theirs. There is an ease to it that pacifies us.

The wide path has the loudest voices, the most followers, the best advertising, and an all-star sales team. It would be easy to forget that the "easy way out" (in which we follow the crowd) is actually a long and desperate route. We all naturally want to fit in, so if everyone around is acting in unison, our natural tendency is to join—even if they are universally acting insane. It is a sad truth that those who follow the crowd usually get lost in it. We might be surrounded by people but we are not truly known. We sit in the crowd, but loneliness knocks at the door.

The ways and patterns of this world (its values and systems) are broken, and they are fading away. Jesus reveals the dichotomy between the wide path and the narrow one—between the road most traveled and life in Him. It seems we have a tough choice to make as human beings.

We can build the Kingdom of Heaven for the good of everyone and the eternal glory of God, or we can build our own little kingdoms, which will be wiped out upon our deaths and washed away into the sands of time. Most of us choose to trade on the lesser economy. Our lives and worship are committed to the popular idols of the well-traveled road of mediocrity.

Jesus understood with crystal clarity that we would have a tough time choosing between living out the life God intended for us and following the broken patterns of the world around us. That is why He gave such clear teachings on the subject. He says that the three-story house, the half million-dollar Porsche, and the iPhone 8 will all be left behind. They stay here on Earth where moths and rust and recycling centers claim all your stuff.

Jesus says that if we gain everything we fantasize about but we compromise our integrity—or live a life apart from Love—we have made a really bad choice. My high school dreams were self-centered and antagonistic toward God's Kingdom, not because wealth is inherently bad, but because we were never meant to worship it. The world, or culture, or mainstream society or whatever you want to call it, moves at a different frequency and thinks in a different manner than it ought to. It functions in an un-godly and sometimes anti-godly way, and it forces us to make a choice.

Jesus reminds us that we cannot have two masters and that we cannot serve both God and money. The trail forks in the road. One is well traveled, and the other has leaves which few steps have trodden black. One is clearly more worthy of our time, but if we still sit torn and undecided at the fork, He reminds us that one of the paths will fade away. You cannot worship both God and money, but your wealth will one day rot and decay. You cannot worship both God and your sex life—they cannot both rule you at the same time—and one will fade away. You cannot worship God and your reputation, and one will soon be forgotten.

On the flip side, you cannot value yourself based on the world's values *and* based on the way that God values you at the same time. You cannot value others as the wide path urges *and* the way that God commands. You cannot treat your friends (or your enemies) the way the world treats them *and* the way that God asks us to treat them. You cannot pursue God's vision for a loving marriage, strong family, or vibrant sex life *and* Hollywood's version at the same time. The two are incompatible—and only one of them satisfies.

You cannot worship yourself, money, or sex as a god and truly worship God at the same time. You cannot hold grudges, hatred, disdain for others and experience the fullness of God at the same time. You cannot love God and hate your enemies at the same time. You cannot commit your life to building your own empire, and live for the Kingdom of Heaven at the same time. We have to make a choice. There are two paths laid out in front of us: one is all about what we can *get* or *gather*, the other is all about what we can *give*—and only one echoes into eternity.

Jesus is inviting us into something unique and full of adventure. He offers us something beautiful and counterintuitive; something rebellious, radical, and refreshing, and that should be reason enough to follow Him, but we should also pause to contemplate this simple spiritual truth: *we will get the fruit of what we worship.* Meaning if we worship things that fade away, then we too may be destined to the same fate. We risk being destroyed along with our little kingdoms. We risk decaying along with our stuff. We should be prepared to fade into nothing along with our forgotten reputations (or the forgotten memory of the sex lives we were enslaved too).

The wide path will die and pass away, and everyone who operates purely on that frequency—who walks only on this path—risks the same fate. We get the fruit of what we worship. This makes sense when we understand that our hearts lie with our treasure—or with the object of our worship—and that the worship of temporal things should never be expected to provide us with anything eternal. The guarantee, however, is that when we walk the road less traveled something glorious awaits us. Not because the path is easy (every Northwesterner knows that the best hikes never are) but because the path is *worth it* and it leads toward something deep and satisfying.

9 The Compass or the Watch?

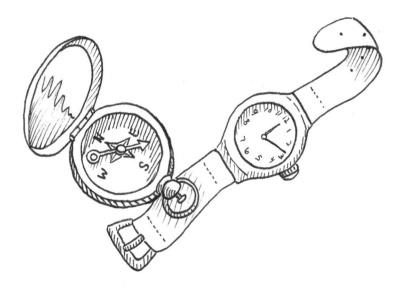

After I graduated from college at the University of Washington in 2008, I worked at Camp Orkila, a YMCA camp in the heart of the San Juan Islands. Situated several hours north of Seattle, the San Juans are some of the most beautiful islands I have ever seen. Nestled between Washington and Canada in the Puget Sound, they are as rugged and wild as you could expect islands to be, at least in the lower forty eight states.

In the spring of 2009, I took a job at Orkila teaching outdoor education classes for middle school students, and to this day it is probably the best place I have ever worked. Every spring the Anacortes ferry brings boatloads of elementary and middle school students out to the islands for the best fieldtrip of their lives. The kids spend a week of "class" in open-air cabins built right on Puget Sound. From their porches they can watch seals hunt the annual salmon runs, and listen to the waves lap against the beach as they fall asleep.

As one of their teachers, I led classes on everything from salmon life cycles, to forests ecosystems, to high ropes courses. One of my favorite classes was the outdoor survival class, in which students were put through wilderness survival scenarios. I am not sure why it was my favorite. I think I was amused by the fact that sixth-grade hormones and the perils of puberty would probably not allow for enough teamwork to survive being lost in the woods.

One of the activities I used to run during survival classes was a mock plane crash. I would take the class out to a field and retell the horrific story of how their plane had crashed unexpectedly and how everyone had miraculously survived except the parents. It was very "Lord of the Flies." The kids would then come crawling and screaming out of the imaginary wreckage and look back with mock horror at the burning pile of metal that used to be their plane.

As the children collected themselves at a safe distance, I would throw a bunch of laminated notecards into the crash site and explain that each notecard represented a resource that would help them survive in the forest. The catch was that they had to "wheel-barrel" each other over to the burning wreckage, selecting one resource at a time to bring it back to safety. The kicker was that the plane was going to explode in a matter of minutes, and they were only allowed to rescue ten items from the wreckage, so they had to choose under pressure which ones to keep and which to discard. The kids would go nuts and start wheel-barreling each other into the burning wreckage to rescue their precious resources.

Each notecard represented a different survival item, and most of them were items you would want if you got lost in the woods: a map, blankets, a compass, and freeze-dried food. There were also some ridiculous items like an elephant, Starbucks coffee, and an iPod. The kids had seen the cards briefly before the exercise started, but only now did they understand the true urgency and importance of the situation. Time was limited and the fire was spreading quickly. After five minutes of chaos I would end the exercise and circle up the group to talk about what had happened.

My favorite part of the exercise was the debrief at the end, in which we tried to analyze the decision-making processes of a bunch of hyped up sixth-graders by asking them to explain the items they had chosen and why. The goal of the exercise (unbeknownst to the students) was not just to learn teamwork but ultimately to select the "ten essentials" for survival, discerning them from the useless items. The ten essentials, for those who don't know, are the ten things you should take with you to increase your chances of survival in the wilderness.[10]

The Ten Essentials:

1. Map
2. Compass
3. Sunglasses and sunscreen
4. Extra clothing
5. Flashlight
6. First-aid supplies
7. Fire starter
8. Matches
9. Knife
10. Extra food

After running the class enough times, I noticed an interesting trend. The students would always successfully choose at least five of the ten essentials. It was always a slightly different set, but they would usually get at least five or six no problem. Most would choose food, water, and extra clothes. Occasionally they would choose the matches, a map, or a first aid kit. But there was one item from the ten essentials that they never chose. I went the whole spring season and never once did a group decide it was important. They generally saw the value in nine of

---

[10]   The exercise assumes you cannot afford a satellite phone or a fully fueled helicopter.

the ten, but there was one that was never selected. The most overlooked of all the essentials was the compass.

The compass was consistently tossed aside and under-valued. It was not eatable or exciting—it didn't have bells and whistles and it couldn't keep you warm at night. It was boring. The kids routinely chose the elephant over the compass. Honestly. Then during debrief they would explain to me why a map was important, how a fire could send smoke signals, and why they were unable to part with their elephant. They regularly reasoned that they could ride the elephant until it died and then eat the meat afterwards. I shuddered at the thought of twelve middle schoolers attempting to dissect and cook an elephant (and I doubt a middle schooler could even get on an elephant's back in the first place) but I appreciated their enthusiasm.

During the debrief sessions it became clear that the students were much more concerned about mounting their elephant and traveling *somewhere* than they were about which direction they were traveling. A compass was of little use to them. They could have been riding the elephant in circles (or in the wrong direction entirely) but this seemed to matter very little. I could not convince them that it was important. It was as if I was speaking a foreign language. They were certain that if they were moving *somewhere*, everything would work out.[11] Accuracy of direction was a boring detail, and group after group would burn the compass and ride the elephant.

---

[11] This was a bit ironic because in a real survival situation the opposite is usually true. It is typically better to stay put, or move very slowly in the right direction, than it is to take off on an elephant deeper into the forest.

The rationale seemed utterly ridiculous, but one day when I was cleaning up after class it struck me that their problem is everyone's problem: we all overlook the compass. Those students were not much different than most Americans. We all look at our watches. We love to figure out how long it will take us to get somewhere in life. But we rarely pause to consider which direction we are traveling. The secret to survival, and the lesson for those middle schoolers, was that the direction you are traveling is more important than how long it takes you to get there.

I think those kids epitomize my generation. We want whatever we want, and we want it *now*. We are a nation that is built on instant gratification and rarely stopping to reflect on which direction we are traveling, which path we are walking, or which road we are on. We are much more concerned with the speedometer. If we are moving quickly, things are good. The problem is that sometimes we take off in an overpriced Porsche going a hundred and twenty miles an hour down the wrong road. Some of us are riding our over-worked elephants in the wrong direction, and I fear that in the process we have become a spiritually stunted people. The potential for spiritual growth in this life is (for all practical purposes) unlimited. It is a process that is never really finished. Although the spiritual speed at which we travel is difficult to gauge, the *direction* in which we travel (and the things that we seek along the way) is far more important than the speed at which we get there. Which means that in order to reclaim the plotline we need to get a compass and forget the watch.

Looking around, it seems that many people in our culture are much more concerned with the speed and ease at which they can attain material wealth, acceptance, or sex, while giving little meaningful thought to what they should actually be pursuing or which direction they should traveling. We often underestimate what a crazy and empowering freedom it is to choose the direction for ourselves. We often forget how badly we need a spiritual compass.

As I read through the Scriptures, I am convinced that God's Spirit was intended to be our inner compass—guiding us moment by moment in the direction we should travel—while simultaneously pointing us back to the Source, and forward toward the horizon of eternity.

But the compass does not appeal to us. We have rejected it completely. Instead, we choose to believe that chasing our undirected desires will bring us freedom. So we rev our engines and go charging down the widest road we can find, excited to see how fast we can go. How drunk can I get? How much money can I amass? How many girls can I sleep with? How many hours can I work? How many followers can I get? How many friends can I amass? How many awards can I win? How many degrees can I earn? But we forget that our instinctual and undirected desires are often corrupted. Apart from God they can drive us to the depths of hell and despair if we allow them to.

Most of us were told at one point or another to "follow your heart," but the age-old adage is sometimes a recipe for disaster, because the Scriptures say that in the absence of God our hearts are often wicked and deceitful. Some people are offended by that idea, but it is not intended as a slam against humanity. In reality, it is a unique insight that was shared for our benefit and flourishing.

Our corrupted desires send us looking for a cheap high and leave us with an ever-increasing sense of emptiness and despair. So we struggle to cover up our despair, drown our sorrows, and bury our conviction by running back to very same vice that brought us despair in the first place. In all likelihood this will either leave us stranded right where we are or cycling into even greater despair, but neither of these are the road you were created to walk. In fact, you were made for something else entirely.

You were made for far more than despair. You were formed for more than shallow happiness. Your destiny, should you choose to claim it, is grander than you could imagine, but too often we forget how to use a compass and choose instead to live by our speedometer. So we push the pedal down . . . straining toward the future . . . only to find ourselves choking on the fumes of a crowded road, fighting off despair and hopelessness as we anxiously grip the wheel and watch our lives slowly tick by on the odometer.

We have this vain hope that somehow our increasing speed will clear the car of its despairing fumes. That if we live life in the fast lane hopelessness will not catch us. But we have misdiagnosed the problem and therefore the solution. The fumes of despair grow thicker, our desires rule us like slaves, and all the while we take great pride in the car we drive and the speed we are able to maintain. We are overjoyed by the status we attain and the people we are pass along the way. *"Who cares if I'm choking on fumes? Check out these rims! I've made it! I am beating everyone at the only game I know how to play! Now why on earth would I hit the brakes and turn it all over to God?"* The idea is repulsive. We would rather choke to death on fumes of despair, traveling a hundred miles an hour down a dead end road. We feed off the respect we get from those around us. It is the only game we know. It is the only direction we know how to travel. We never stopped to check the compass.

Too often we chase down the despair of our empty dreams, rejecting the God we sense will only slow us down. *"No one will respect me if I believe in God,"* we think, *"that's not the direction I've chosen. That will only derail my plans."* As we stand at the fork in the road, we are often more intrigued by the idea of riding a dying elephant down the wide path than walking on foot down the only path worth taking.

Growing up I did not give much thought to the road less traveled, but once you get a taste of it mediocrity ceases to satisfy. We no longer want to trade on the lesser economy. We no longer chase down the fruits of lesser worship. We no longer charge down the wide path, gloating over the people we pass on the freeway. God changes all of that.

For most of my life I could not believe in a higher power. The concept of God seemed both silly and dangerous, but it's funny how things change over time, and it turns out we have to change over time because we are human and we are all traveling somewhere. We are all traveling down one path or another, and the path we walk will shape us as along away. Today, things are different. When I look out my window today I see a new world—a different world from the one I thought I knew before. Today I know a higher power. I have tasted it, I have been graced by it, and it was so unexpected and counterintuitive that my world was turned upside-down . . . and rebuilt into something beautiful.

Today I stumble down the road less traveled.

10 Waiting for the Dawn

Back when I was in high school—before I became a Christian—I didn't care for Christians much. From a distance I caught glimpses of rigid doctrines and illogical stories which I neither understood nor believed. I saw preachers who seemed to be trying to convince themselves and their listeners of some improbable crap that they did not actually buy. I saw self-righteous people who thought they were good and I was bad simply because they went to church and I did not—as if they had clocked in and clocked out on a Sunday and somehow they had become righteous and good while the rest of us were less-than-worthy. I saw phony-looking guys giving sermons on TV that I just could not stand to listen to. I viewed the South as being the harbor for both Christianity and racism, and because I did not believe that anyone who was racist had any significant moral or intellectual capacities, I went on to assume that there was a correlation between the two. I thought religion made people closed-minded, bigoted, and completely not fun. I saw the Church as a house full of people who bought into an illusion simply because they were confused about their own dull lives—but I think it was worse than that.

Back then I think I actually wanted Christians to fail. I wanted them to see and experience things that would force them to give up the illusions they have been sold and get back to being normal again. I wanted them to come back to reality.

It seemed as though they had designed a story and a belief system that was so abstract and distant that it could not be disproved. Yet because they had placed it beyond the reach of logic and science it was now so aloof and far off that it gave them no real benefit, and the rest of us were unable to talk them out of it. I concluded it was simply a clever system of beliefs that could not be decisively disproven, but could not be truly validated either. I figured if there was enough weight and pressure put on Christians they would abandon their crazy ideas and they would stop bothering people so much. I guess part of me just wanted to live in peace without being challenged.

I had a good life and I had no reason at all to step into a church and listen to some boring old man tell me a bunch of weird ideas that I would have to force myself to believe (assuming that were even possible in the first place). I thought that if I wanted to have faith and go to heaven—according to their ideas—I would have to basically convince myself to believe dull, uninspiring, made-up stories for the next seventy years until I died.

It sounded pretty terrible, but I knew a handful of respectable people who went to church, and part of me was looking for something greater than my own little life, so I must admit that once or twice I actually considered what it would be like to force myself to believe in God just to be a part of something. But the idea never lasted more than two days. Perhaps part of me even wanted to have faith, but I assumed it was a pointless exercise. Sooner or later my logic would get the best of me and crush whatever fragile faith I was trying to muster. After all, it seemed that no one could really face the logic of it head on and still have faith.

As I got closer, I heard a lot of weird stuff about this guy named Jesus and His death and how we were bad people and we were supposed to follow Him. I heard we were supposed to go to church and be like sheep or something. "*Sheep?!*" I thought, "*Those dumb, oblivious animals?*

Are we to put our minds to sleep and just comply without question? What animal is more helpless and stupid than a sheep? Maybe religious people were just being dumb because they were told to be dumb and they were too dumb to question the command."

Surely I would eventually question some belief that was not to be questioned and get myself into trouble. Religious beliefs (as I understood them) were dictated to the congregation by pastors and the people were told to accept them as true by faith. So in a sense faith meant "go to church and don't ask questions." Questions signal doubt or concern and those seemed to be the opposite of faith. Even at a young age I valued inquiry and the power of asking big questions which made religious faith seem very off-putting.

Surely this whole "Jesus" thing was not for me. I was freethinking and independent; I liked standing out, charting my own path, and walking to the beat of my own drum. I did not like religious people—particularly Christians—and I did not see much of the glory of God in the world, if He existed at all. I heard a lot of passionate rhetoric about following God or going to hell and I wasn't sure if it was better to fight back or just walk away.

Maybe I would become a Buddhist monk, I thought. That would be cool. Nobody has a problem with Buddhist monks; they just sit around and meditate on peace. They seemed like spiritual people, and being spiritual seemed like a good thing. For the most part I viewed myself as a heartfelt and "spiritual" person. I mean, who can slam the door on all of human spirituality? Even as an atheist, I knew that some part of me felt "spiritual." Most of us sense that we have this capacity; it's just a matter of figuring out how to bring it to life. Mine first came to life in nature.

I spent a lot of time outdoors as a kid. My parents both grew up in Ohio, and after they got married they moved to Detroit, which is where I was born. My parents were dirt-poor back then, so we basically lived in the ghetto. I was too young to remember but I still like telling people I was born in the ghetto in Detroit, as if they will respect me for it. I didn't have to scavenge for my own food, and I am pretty sure the diapers are just as soft in Detroit, but I was less than two years old when my parents moved us out to Washington State to start a new life, so I don't really remember.

My parents moved out West for the mountains, and as a result our family spent a lot of time exploring. I went on my first camping trip when I was a few months old and we never really stopped. By the time my brother, sister, and I could walk we were hiking. We camped all over Washington and Oregon, exploring their beaches and climbing their mountains. One summer I think we camped every single weekend. We would get home, unpack what needed to be washed, then repack everything in order have it ready for the next weekend.

We don't have much American history in the Northwest. We don't have the Liberty Bell or famous statues from France. We don't have the White House or the Washington Monument. Our oldest buildings are not very old. But I think that is the trade-off you get for living on the West Coast. I may not be able to spell Massechewsetts, I sometimes get Philadelphia confused for a state, I cannot place Maryland on a map, and we don't have any monuments, but it's worth it because we have some breath-taking landscapes.

We have mountains so tall that you get altitude sickness trying to climb them. We have old growth forests that spill down the foothills toward the Pacific Ocean, where orca whales hunt migrating salmon. We have mile long beaches, endless hiking trails, and more wilderness than you could explore in a lifetime.

My family spent years going on adventures in the Great Northwest, but of all the dozens of places we got to explore growing up, the Olympic Mountains were my favorite. The Olympic mountain range dominates the Olympic Peninsula, (a relatively unpopulated area along Washington's Coast) which is surprisingly difficult to reach for most Washingtonians. As a result, most people from Seattle or Tacoma hike on other mountains, leaving the Olympics wild and untouched.

Olympic National Park is the biggest piece of unbroken wilderness in the continental United States, and few places can compare with its beauty. As a child, those mountains were the equivalent of giant temples, buzzing with holy energy.

When I was young I didn't care much for religion. My church was out there. It was Washington's mountains, and Oregon's Pacific Ocean. It was the beauty of a creek winding through an old growth forest, or a storm rolling in across the sea. Never did I feel more inspired—or closer to the presence of the divine—than when I was standing on one of those mountain ridges, looking out over snowy peaks and alpine forests that seem to stretch out in every direction. I will never forget the feeling of that fresh mountain air rushing up the ridge as I was overwhelmed by the beauty and power that surrounded me. My skin would tingle with goose bumps, and I had the sensation that my heart was being made new again. As if I was being bathed in something pure and refreshing. There was nothing quite like it.

Even today when I stand in a place of true natural beauty I can practically hear organs playing. There is really something spiritual about a place of unspoiled wilderness. There is an aspect of nature so profound and life giving that it seems to escape any words I might prescribe to it. There is a beauty there that moves the heart. Architects can build stunning Cathedrals, but none of them comes close to matching Mt. Rainer in its beauty.

Throughout my childhood, nature was a place of such deep peace and inspiration that I came to associate nature with spirituality. Growing up camping and hiking, I would regularly experience moments of sheer joy and ecstasy in nature. I also had unique introspective moments when it felt as if something in my heart were coming to life. I can only describe as these moments as spiritual experiences, because I have no other words to describe them. I was captivated by the power of that beautiful world, and it seemed as if we were designed to be connected to it. It felt as if we were supposed to stand out there in the wild places and just listen. It seemed as if there was some missing part of us out there, waiting to be rediscovered.

Standing on top of one of those mountain ridges, I would feel a peace and power wash over me that was unlike anything I had ever tasted. There was such a deep mystery there—something that made my veins buzz with excitement and my heart swell with joy. The mountains and forests of the Northwest left a lasting impact on me, and I guess you could say the first thing I really believed in was the spiritual power of nature. If the "Spirituality of

Nature" were a church, I would have joined at age eight. I regarded nature with a sense of reverence that was unmatched by anything and that certainly included church. I had limited experiences with church growing up, and each experience turned out to be dull and boring. I was not entertained by what was preached, and my heart was not stirred by the experience. It was very much a *"hold-your-breath-and-try-to-get-through-this-awkward-situation-as-quickly-as-you-can"* type of experience. Half the time I did not see the relevance of the material, and the other half I did not understand the material at all (nor did I care to find out).

My early visits led me to believe that church was a somewhat dull and mindless place, while childhood exploration taught me that nature was a place to experience the raw power of life. Out there I sensed the deep and simple beauty of the world, and I felt moved by the real and powerful forces that people were probably looking for in church. It made me wonder if church was not a misguided experiment in inspiration that fell flat. I figured the Church must have missed something. It was as if they were trying to milk inspiration from their outdated stories and stuffy pews. It seemed as if they were selling second-rate manufactured beauty to an unsuspecting public that had yet to taste the real thing. It seemed to me that church people would be better off just climbing a mountain—then they might taste real inspiration and leave their pre-packaged and phony alternatives behind.

For the most part I started my journey of faith as a very skeptical person. I only believed and trusted in what I could see under a microscope—*unseen* was the equivalent of *unreal*. But I think the Olympics changed that for me. I think Mt. Rainer made me think twice. I had stood on those mountains and *experienced* something. What I felt escaped words, but it felt bigger and richer than my individual life. Something happened out there that opened up my mind to new possibilities and smashed my hopes of self-worship to a thousands pieces.

I think God was speaking to me on those mountains. I think He was tugging on my heart and whispering to me long before I knew that God had a name. I think that is why (in the end) science did not become my religion. Because when I stood on those mountain ridges and electric energy would ripple down my spine and buzz in my veins I knew there was something special happening in our seemingly ordinary world. I knew that there was something real in the unseen—something that had substance and weight—and that epiphany left the door open for a world of possibilities.

11 Breaking the Horizon

G rowing up I was always the shy observant kid. You probably do not know many of us, because we are typically shy and observant, meaning that we rarely catch people's attention. If we are truly committed to the craft, you never learn our names. Throughout elementary school I was outgoing enough, but by the time I got to middle school I hardly said a word. I slowly started opening up in high school, but it was not until my senior year that I truly started to emerge from my introverted cave.

After I graduated from high school I moved out of my parents' house in Lakewood, Washington and moved up to Seattle to start college at the University of Washington. By some miracle I underwent a personal metamorphosis. By the time I reached UW I was a downright extrovert. Suddenly I wanted to talk to anyone who would listen, try anything that would not kill me, and meet everyone I could. It was at UW that I met Jesus.

Part way into the school year UW held a student club fair. There were close to forty thousand students at UW, so you can imagine how big the club fair was. There was a club for everything under the sun. If you like ballet or hip-hop dancing there was a club for that. If you like writing poems on the back of napkins and sharing them out loud, there was a club for that too. If you like fighting with foam swords in public places, there was a club for that. I was into getting drunk with my roommates and playing Halo, and they did not have a club for that, so I decided not to join a club.

I had no interest in exploring the fair. The only issue was that the event filled the entire student union building, and then came spilling out onto the lawn. Which meant that in order to walk from the dorms to class I had to walk right through it. I remember passing by rows of tables with my headphones blaring. All the while wondering if my roommate Erick would beat me back to the dorms so we could play Halo on his Xbox. I glanced around at some of the club tables as I passed by, and in the process I accidently made eye contact with one of the guys behind the tables, who was quick to give me a big smile. I immediately shot a glance down at the club sign and saw that it was a Christian club. I proceeded to walk right by him and on toward the dorms. Then something happened.

I remember stopping dead in my tracks, for no reason at all. I just stood there, while a constant stream of students flowed around me. I felt like a stubborn rock in the middle of a river, and as I stood there I felt something on my heart in that moment, something I cannot fully describe or articulate. I had the strange sense that I was supposed to do something, and I knew exactly I was needed to do. I was supposed to go back and talk to that guy. In my typical shyness I would have kept walking, but I was different now. I was a new man, an extrovert, and I was not going to back down from a challenge.

I slowly swallowed my pride, turned around, and walked back to the table. I introduced myself to the young man who had smiled at me, and he introduced himself as Christian (yes, that was really his name). After a brief conversation he signed me up for their kick-off BBQ, which over the course of a few weeks turned into a weekly men's Bible study. I had never been to a Bible Study before— and I had never owned a Bible—so I just showed up.

I really liked the guys in the Bible study and I quickly decided that I was going to stay, mostly because I was willing to try anything that wouldn't kill me, and I was fairly certain a Bible study wouldn't kill me. So I kept showing up, but I did not have a clue what they were talking about. I was intrigued enough to stay, but confused enough to have almost no idea what was going on. In the end, I resolved to reveal my ignorance by asking lots of questions. I mean *lots* of questions.

Truth be told, I probably ran those guys through the gauntlet, but I needed to grasp what they believed, so I just kept asking. The irony is that people think asking questions is at odds with having faith, when in reality we cannot discover anything worth finding unless we are willing to ask really tough questions. Besides, what choice did I have? I was not going to sit in silence for an hour and a half every Tuesday night and pretend like I knew what was going on. All I could do was strain forward in an attempt to grasp the story that had captured their hearts.

When I first came to the story of God, I did not understand it at all. It was completely foreign to me. I was stumbling around half blind through strange tales about shepherds having visions, and trying to follow the law of a God I had never heard of. I was catching little glimpses of the God who supposedly loved people, but it didn't make sense. I had already written my own story about reality that involved scientific laws, the quest for happiness, and not much else. This new idea—this new way of thinking, breathing, and viewing the universe—was completely uncharted territory. I had spent nineteen years exploring and investigating. I had written my map of reality and I knew how to navigate it. I understood people and how to navigate systems in order to be successful. I had everything I needed, and no reason at all to go looking for new continents.

I thought I already knew everything I needed to know, and God was not on the map. In fact, I did not leave room for God to exist at all, let alone for there to be any comprehensive and accurate theory about His nature. Tuesday night Bible study was a challenging and perplexing way to spend my time, but I just had to know if there was any truth in what they were saying. I had to know what sustained them, and the longer I stayed, the more I began to understand.

The Bible tells a striking story about God. It is not terribly complicated; I think most six year olds can understand it and live it out. It is not rocket science, but it is unexpected; it is not overly complex, but it is counterintuitive. Coming in blind, it truly defied all my expectations, and it was nothing like I had originally assumed. The story of God is a story worth sharing, and the Bible is more fascinating than I ever would have dreamed.

** The Bible in few short pages **

The Scriptures claim that our reality (and perhaps time itself) started when God created the material universe, and eventually the earth and all the living things that inhabit it, which eventually gets us to you and me. People get really caught up on the timeline, but the point is that the God of the Bible designed mitochondria and set galaxies in motion and He has an abundance of love for us that never fails. He wrote the code imbedded in our DNA and wrote the formula for gravity, and He has you on His heart. He is the Source of all things.

From this God—from this source with a capital S—came a staggering array of beautiful landscapes, black holes, and songbirds. He is the Source of supernovas, humpback whales, snow-capped mountains, and ten thousand varieties of tropical fish. After creating it all, when the time was right, He prepared a special place for humanity, and brought them up out of nothing—filling them with life, giving them identity, and bringing them into the unique time and place we call "the garden."

In the beginning, we had incredible intimacy with God. He ruled and reigned, and there was no death, no evil, nothing that the Bible calls sin. There was no depression, heartache, abuse, or poverty. There was no fear and no crushing sense of loneliness. There were no parking tickets, splinters, or morning breath. There was just awesome food, great sex, meaningful work, and (most importantly) an incredible and unprecedented intimacy with our Creator. There was a palpable and deep sense of peace, which the Hebrews called "shalom." Shalom is not just the absence of war, it is the presence of overwhelming peace. Shalom is more than just a ceasefire, it is absolute fulfillment in every dimension of your being—which is almost impossible for us to understand because we have not experienced it yet. In the Garden of Eden there was shalom, but it did not last very long.

Right off the bat, people choose to be their own gods, to rule their own lives, and to use their free will to reject God in disobedience and mistrust. We thought we knew better. We thought God was holding out on us, and we wanted more for ourselves. So the people who were made in God's image rejected the life that God had in store for them, setting in motion a world full of brokenness, pain, death, sin, entropy, and darkness. That is the world you were born into, and the rebellion continues today. For most of humanity, it is all we know. It is the normative human condition, as if it were built in our fallen DNA.

The natural result of rebellion and sin against God is isolation and eventual death: spiritual, emotional, physical death. Sin is like gravity: it naturally splits, fractures, and pulls us away. We now live in a world defined and ruled by entropy, where our natural inclination is to depart from the Source of all life and decay in our self-centeredness.

All the people who originally rejected God made babies, and then those babies grew up and had babies, and after enough years had passed God decided to do something special with the human project. When a major flood failed to bring the remnant of humanity back into shalom, God made it clear He was opening a new chapter in the redemption of humanity, in which He called out a people group that He was going to use in a special way. He decided to create a unique nation that He could use to bless every other nation on Earth. The plan was for this "community of blessing" to represent God's heart to the world. They were to live in such a beautiful and distinct way that the whole world would be drawn back to God and back toward the peace and shalom they had lost

So God took an enslaved people in Egypt and (as promised) He freed them. God literally set them free, they hardly had to lift a finger. Today we know this liberated ethnic group as ancient Israel. He told Israel that through them He was going to bless the world like crazy, and bring His Kingdom way of life to Earth. It was through Israel that God revealed His power to redeem and restore. It was to Israel that He first revealed His heart and His Name.

God was speaking, moving, and guiding. He was slowly revealing His nature to a lost and hurting world, and good things were starting to happen.

Beautiful things were stirring in and through this people group, but the problem was they were still human. They still had this rebellious bent. They were still restless, unsatisfied, and stubborn, and what God gave them— which was abundantly more than they deserved—often was not enough for them, so they continuously walked away. The story of Israel is, in many ways, the story of humanity. It is the story of what happens when the irresistible force of God's love (and His relentless desire to bless us) meet the immovable object of the self-centered human heart.

What was true of Adam and Eve is true of us: we do not want to be blessed by God on His terms; we would rather try to bless ourselves. We do not want to come under God's Kingship; we would rather be our own kings. Israel did what all of us do—they went their own way, rejecting God all over again. Some worshipped other gods, some worshipped money, and some worshipped sex, (not much has changed in the last three thousand years) but God kept pursuing them, calling them back, and inviting them to belong to Him.

It turns out that when we make up our own story about the universe, we end up really hurting each other and screwing things up pretty badly, and every time Israel screwed up and hit rock bottom they would cry out to God, and He would answer them and bring them back into a place of blessing.

The same cycle kept repeating itself again and again, and people (even well-meaning religious people) kept operating outside of God's heart, until finally something extraordinary happened. The full genius of God's plan to bless the world was finally revealed. A man came onto the scene—a man who claimed to be God in the flesh. Remember the God who created everything and brought it into being? The One who breathed the material universe into existence? Well, He clothed himself in flesh and blood—adding humanity to His divinity—and in a confusing turn of events He confounded us all by being born as a baby boy.

The truth is that we should have seen it coming, because God had been telling His people for thousands of years about a Messiah (or Anointed King) who was going to come and crush evil to usher in a New Kingdom. It just did not happen the way we had anticipated. The entire event was not overly complicated or unforeseeable, just counterintuitive.

This man—this "God-man"—was an average looking man from a less-than-average little town. He did not have an army or political power. He was not popular, even among the religious elite. He did not have money or powerful connections. He did not have a high quality education or even all-star parents. But He had a message.

The message was one of love and redemption. In its simplest form He said "repent and believe, because the Kingdom of Heaven is at hand"—or said another way: "renew your hearts and minds and redraw your life maps because the Kingdom of God is at your fingertips; it is breaking into your reality even now."

The Spirit of God rested so fully on this man that He was more complete and arguably more *human* than any of us will ever be this side of death. He was so full of God's

Spirit that He was able to speak the words of our forgotten God—reminding humanity who she is, who she was, and how God is going to redeem her. He reminded humanity of our forgotten plotline and our lost purpose. He revealed ever-more fully God's heart for creation.

Finally, when the time came and He had delivered His message—shaking up the social and religious order and turning our cramped narcissistic perspectives upside down—He went to die.

Most of us do not understand all the reasons that Jesus had to die. I certainly don't. And I guess, strictly speaking, He didn't have to die at all. But He wanted to. The Scriptures say it was for the joy set before Him that He went to the cross. If you know the story of Jesus' death, you know that no sane and conscious human being would find joy in it because crucifixion is (to this day) the most brutal and humiliating way to die.

But I think Jesus found joy in it because He knew He was accomplishing something. He knew He was about to do the unthinkable. He was about to turn sin and shame and evil on its head, bringing many sons and daughters back into the fold of God's love. He knew that He was about to stand in our place for our sins, tearing down the wall separating us from God's Spirit, fulfilling a promise to Abraham and unleashing a new era of the Kingdom of God right here and now, in this reality.

I think that is why He endured the cross; the horrific beatings, the shame, and the crown made of thorns. I think that is why He endured the internal bleeding and let them drive nails through some of the most sensitive nerve centers in His body. The brutality of the cross is shocking, but what is far more shocking is the message that it conveys. When I look at the cross, I am brought to my knees and face to face with the truth: *God would do anything for us.* It is shocking that any human being would face crucifixion for the sake of another human being. It is even more shocking that the God of the universe would face crucifixion for you.

So the man with no money, no home, and no children breathed His last while nailed to a tree, and then lay brutalized and lifeless in a stone tomb in the ancient Near East. That average looking man with the average sounding name from an average little town was laid to rest. His followers wandered home defeated, abandoning their hope at the sight of their lifeless "Messiah." Days passed by as the people mourned.

And then something unthinkable happened. This unthinkable event was not unforeseen, but it was even more counterintuitive. A life, energy, and Spirit which defies our very imaginations, which outstrips our capacity to dream, which outpaces our logic and our cognitive thoughts, came pouring into that tomb and orchestrated an event that would launch that obscure Nazarene to the very center of human spirituality and discourse, making Him the most culturally significant person ever to walk the earth. An event happened which unleashed a new way of life right in the middle of our entropy-governed reality:

Jesus came back from the dead.

He rose again to eat, breath, laugh, love, and walk the earth. That average looking guy from a Podunk town is now talked about in every nation on Earth, because He rose up from the grave. In fact, I would argue if he had not risen from the dead *you would not know His name.*

I used to think the resurrection of Jesus was religious fantasy or cultural myth, but it turns out we have as much evidence establishing the resurrection as we do for any other fact in ancient history,[12] which means we have to reach for new ways of understanding what happened that fateful morning. I think something happened in that tomb that modern day science cannot explain. After lying lifeless for several days, that old, worthless pile of flesh was caught up and incorporated into something brand new.

Resurrection might sound like something out of zombie movie, but Jesus was not raised from the dead in a zombie apocalypse run-for-your-basement sort of way. He resurrected in a form no one expected to see this side of eternity. Somehow He came back more whole—He had a new body governed by new properties and controlled by new rules. It had elements of the old, but it was completely new. The old parameters (including some of the laws of physics) no longer bound His body. His new body behaved in ways that His old body never could, and people took notice. At one point He walked right through a locked door, and when the disciples accused Him of being a ghost, He sat down and ate their lunch as they watched. Everyone was stunned. Nothing like this had ever happened before. There was no frame of reference to explain what was taking place. There were no scientific laws that could make sense of the situation. The resurrection shocked the world.

And this is where the story gets really crazy, because in the wake of Jesus resurrection God promised something

---

[12] A fact that even the world's greatest atheists cannot explain.

unthinkable. Most of us cannot get past the fact that God exists to begin with. We are stuck on the first verse of the Bible. Those of us who do believe He exists are forced to wrestle with the fact that God loves us, pursues us, and that He came as a man to set the world right again. Most of us struggle to accept that when Jesus was on the cross He was accomplishing something for *us*. But even if your mind has not rejected this fantastic story altogether you are not finished yet because it gets even more shocking. The unthinkable climax of the story of the Scriptures is that God is going to remake the entire universe in the same way he remade the lifeless body that lay in that tomb. God is building a new Kingdom, and all who belong to Him will be *resurrected into it*.

God promises to take the entire cosmos and make them new again—incorporating parts of the old into the new, but ultimately creating something with new properties governed by new rules. A place where the constraints and limits of this world are left behind and even the natural laws of this universe are altered and changed. No longer will it be ruled by entropy, futility, and sin. God is restoring everything back to Himself—back to the Garden of Eden—except this time God is going to create an eternal place centered around a garden-like city. The Scriptures creatively refer to this reality as the Age to Come.

It turns out God created at least two realms of experience: one heavenly and one earthly. In this moment He exists now most clearly in the heavenly realm, but the ultimate hope we carry—His promise to us—is that He will one day return to Earth and unite the two. God will come to restore all creation, dragging heaven with Him as He comes. One day heaven and Earth will collide. This future

MATT DEISEN

reality is what we call the Kingdom of God, the Kingdom of Heaven, or the New Heavens and New Earth. Some Christians end up thinking that the ultimate destination is heaven. However the goal was never for us to escape Earth for heaven: the climax of God's story is the moment the two become one.

It turns out that heaven and Earth were made for each other; like two chemicals longing to spark a reaction. Like the vinegar and baking soda of our little paper mache volcanoes. The stored potential energy, the anticipation of that grand collision, and the prophesied result of that radical reaction is what fuels us with hope.

Life is an unexpected phenomenon, and the original creation was a shocking and incomprehensible act, but re-creation promises to be just as provocative. The rebirth will be just as radical as the first birth, though perhaps even easier to accept. In fact, I would argue that the jump between this age and the Age to Come is actually less shocking and easier to grasp than original creation. In other words, if we can grasp the sheer unexpected and nearly impossible act of original creation—the process of going from *nothing* to everything—and we can further accept that it had a Source, then a theory of re-creation and the recycling and renewing of what already exists is not so difficult to comprehend. Believing that our world will be wrapped up and incorporated into something new—that heaven will come crashing into Earth—actually requires less of a logical jump than accepting original creation, and it is only difficult to comprehend on any level because we have yet to see it.

Creating life out of nothing seems to take more creative energy than renewing it. Original creation actually seems less logical, and (strictly speaking) harder to believe than re-creation. We only believe in original creation because we are standing in it, and the provocative promise of Jesus is that we are not standing in the final product . . . and that all who follow Him one day will.

This is the Gospel, and the brilliant thing about this Gospel and the God who announces it that He resonates in the hearts of small children, and simultaneously delights and stumps our greatest intellectual thinkers. Our visionaries and dreamers cannot fully grasp Him, He confounds the wisdom of the wise, and we all stand like children before Him. You could get lost in this mystery for the rest of your life, and those who abandon themselves in pursuit of Him may very well find themselves exploring and enjoying the mystery of God for many countless centuries to come. This is the story of the Scriptures, and the brilliant thing about this story is that it's your story . . . and it's not finished yet.

12 Shifting Gears

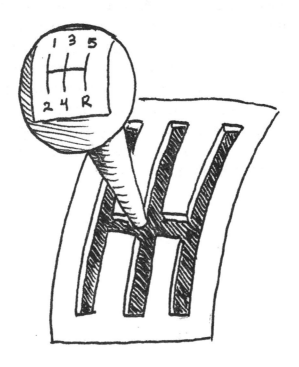

I once bought a stick shift without knowing it.

It was 2013 when I got my first car. I mean, I had driven a car before, but I had never owned one. A lot of kids in my neighborhood got their first car when they turned sixteen. I got mine at twenty-seven. Throughout high school there was always an extra family car in the driveway. When I graduated high school and moved to Seattle to start college, I found I could get around just fine using public transportation.

The city bus is hard to get used to at first, but once you do it can actually be pretty enjoyable. Luckily two of my favorite past times are reading books and people watching, and there is plenty of opportunity for both on the city bus. After graduating college I stayed in Seattle and continued to bus everywhere and read really good books, until eventually I moved to Portland to start law school. Portland also has great buses, and to top it off I had an orange bike, so it wasn't until half way through law school that I asked to borrow the extra family car again. My parents graciously allowed me to borrow it under the condition that I pass it on to my younger brother when I graduated.

In May 2013, I graduated from law school and my student loan money was all but gone. I was nearly broke, and it was time to give the family car back. With fifteen hundred dollars in my bank account and a whole summer of unemployment ahead of me, I needed to find a creative way to get around while studying for the bar exam. So I decided to look for a motorcycle. It probably was not the best idea in a place where it rains eight months a year, but I figured a motorcycle would be cheaper than a car, and I was hard pressed for cash. After asking around for a couple weeks, a friend of mine reached out and offered to sell me his motorcycle for a thousand dollars, which was just about the most I could afford to spend. It was probably worth twice that much (and he knew it) but I told him I still needed a few days to think it over. In the meantime I asked my friend "Stan the Man" to help me find a better deal.

In July 2012, Jake (my road bike friend) married Kate. Kate's dad is the man—so much so that we sometimes call him Stan the Man, because Stan can do anything. He can build houses with his bare hands, fix anything that can break, and build cars from spare parts. Stan is the manliest guy I know, and he seems even manlier in my eyes because I can't fix a leaky faucet, let alone make sense of a car engine. Stan is a great guy to have in your corner, not only because he knows a lot about everything, but also because he is also one of the best negotiators I know. Stan gets people to sell things that are not for sale, which basically makes him the negotiating equivalent of a Jedi knight.

I told Stan that I was willing to spend up to a thousand dollars on a vehicle, and asked if he knew of a good car or motorcycle that I could buy. He told me he would keep his eyes out and let me know if he found anything. I assumed nothing would come up in the course of a few days, but sure enough two days later Stan was running errands when he noticed a car with several parking tickets on it. He immediately called the owner and asked to buy the car. Stan's the type of guy who will do that—who will ask to buy things that are not for sale. I figured he would just get turned down a lot, but you would not believe the bargains he finds. Stan got the owner on the phone and requested the privilege of buying his neglected vehicle . . .

"That's funny you called!" the owner replied, "I was just about to put in on craigslist for seventeen hundred."

"Sorry that's out of our price range," Stan responded, "I am buying this car for a kid who just graduated from college and we can only afford to pay a thousand."

Stan immediately hung up on him (I do not have the guts to do stuff like that, which is why I call Stan in the first place). Sure enough, ten minutes later the owner called back, "If you've got cash now, I'll sell it for a thousand," he said, "I could use the money."

Stan called me immediately and said he could get me a car for a thousand dollars, with new tires, new brakes, and a smooth running engine, and I told him to buy it. I was so excited I forgot to ask any questions, and I hung up the phone buzzing with enthusiasm. *No rainy motorcycle rides for me; I would be riding in style!*

It was not until two days later that I learned the make, model, and color of the car . . . and the fact that it's a stick shift. The car I bought was a little white Infiniti G20, which, despite being twenty years old, ran beautifully. The car was pretty beat up, but completely lovable. Sure, it was missing the grill and the hood did not close all the way, but I could not have been happier. My issue was not the age of the car, or the missing grill, but the fact that I had no idea how to drive a stick shift.

Luckily Jake drives a stick and he showed me the ropes. We went for a ride, and I got to ask him tons of questions about shifting gears, what a clutch does, and why I was stalling every time I attempted to go from zero to five miles an hour. Jake even let me stall his car around the block a few times. I had no idea what I was doing, and I was a little embarrassed. To be honest, the whole experience felt like being back in my old Bible Study. Learning to drive a stick shift felt unnatural and difficult. I just had to step out with determination and do the only thing I knew how to do: ask tons of questions and stumble my way through it.

I spent the next few days stalling my little G20 at just about every intersection in Portland. On more than one occasion I found myself at the front of the line at a red light and I stalled my little car through the entire green light and into the next cycle! The whole experience was terribly embarrassing. The light would turn green, I would stall the car (*dang!*) and then throw my emergency lights on. I would then turn the car off and back on again, only to stall all over again as disgruntled drivers honked restlessly behind me and as my cheeks flushed red with embarrassment. It got to the point where I pretty much learned to put the emergency lights on whenever I buckled my seatbelt. I did not have a clue what I was doing. But at least I was going somewhere, and I was determined to figure it out as I went. It was only a matter of time before I started getting the hang of it. As soon as I did, I loved it! Once I learned how to shift gears, I never wanted to go back.

In my experience, learning to drive a stick was remarkably like coming to faith in Jesus, because my process of coming to faith was a gradual one, and I took things one slow step at a time. I once would have labeled myself an atheist. I did not know God, see God at work, or understand the concept of God (or the people that followed Him). No one could prove to me that God existed and it all seemed a bit foolish, but at some point I realized that there really *could* be something grander and bigger out there, and I guess at that point I was really agnostic, not atheist. At some point the Olympic Mountains got the better of me, and (spiritually speaking) this was the equivalent of first gear. I was moving somewhere, but it was slow. You can only get so far in first gear.

I was trying to stay open-minded and objective, but I still had not seen enough to make me think there was a God. It just did not seem plausible that there was all this life-defining truth that I could not see, touch, or readily access. The engine was straining to move the car forward, and my heart was longing for something more, but I was maxing out the capacity of first gear. I was maxing out the spiritual growth you can experience by simply believing there is probably something bigger than yourself.

For me, shifting into first gear started with my heart whispering that there was something more out there—that we are more than the result of random chance in a vacuum. My gut told me this was no longer an adequate theory. The evidence was stacking up in favor of something far more grand. I began to sense that nature, beauty, love, and laugher were inspired by something more beautiful and complex than themselves. It seemed plausible— and perhaps even necessary—that some force or power brought them into being and gave birth to them.

Eventually I was able to see that this "something" was not a force in the sense that gravity is a force, but rather a higher power or energy—something deeper and more profound than the forces of nature or physics. For a skeptical, science-minded person, this was a mind blowing and challenging conclusion to arrive at. Just like mastering my new car, first gear was the hardest to handle, but

I was encountering something greater than the human mind, more powerful than human thoughts, and more overwhelming than human emotions.

First Gear: *There is something greater than me in the universe.*

Next came the epiphany that this higher power had beauty and creative power, and that it was not simply a force of physics, or a heartwarming aspect of nature, but it had a *personality.* For me, this was the equivalent of shifting into second gear because it opened my mind to the idea that this creative force could be the source of life. The Creator—or what we call God"— is an all-powerful Being that actually gave birth to the universe. Armed with this belief, I was going places, and the car was gaining momentum.

From there I was able to accept that God did not just create the universe, but obviously humanity as well, as we are a physical part of the physical universe. God made life itself possible, and made light when there was only darkness. The universe is like a song that God sang into motion. He created the stage on which we act, setting us in motion and giving us the capacity to think, ponder, search, and dream, and as I accepted that this universe has a Creator, I shifted into second gear. You can do a lot more in second gear then you can in first, and as I shifted, I felt a new sense of excitement and freedom.

Second Gear: *God exists and God created.*

As soon as you shift into second gear, things start to happen. It was not long before I came to believe that

God did not create the universe only to abandon it; that He is not a cold, distant, unknowable mystery. In fact, the life-altering truth about God is that *He wants to be known.* There is ongoing involvement and interaction between Creator and creation. It turns out that God has not abandoned this place. In fact, He never left.

Of course this raised the question of what this ever-present God was like, and how He viewed the world He created, and eventually I came to believe that the personal force we call God actually loves us. This realization represented third gear, and all of a sudden my faith truly had speed and momentum. You can go almost anywhere in third gear, at least locally.

Third gear for me was the idea that God actively loves us, not only by giving us a home that naturally produces food and fresh air, but also by giving joy, guidance, strength, love, wisdom and grace—by engaging in an continuous loving relationship with us. God loves us by forgiving us, speaking to us, and giving us an account of His character and activity in the world. He gives us a small but powerful glimpse of His nature and His plan for the redemption of the universe. It may be the tip of the iceberg in terms of exposing the nature of an infinite and everlasting God, but it is powerful enough to change a human life from top to bottom, and as lives are changed, so is the world.

Third Gear: *God loves us.*

After reaching third gear, I plateaued for a number of years before finally stumbling upon my next epiphany: Jesus was a real man, who actually lived, breathed, and walked among people. He was actually here—not as a part of some fairy tale or legend, but as historical reality. I am not even aware of a legitimate scholar who would challenge the fact that Jesus was a real man in history, but for some reason I had placed him in the same category as the Easter Bunny, Santa Clause, and other inspiring mythical characters. To acknowledge His existence, and His potential role within the faith I professed was progress.

Even after acknowledging the historical Jesus, there was a period of about two years in late high school and early college when I believed in a Judeo-Christian God, and probably even considered myself a Christian, but still maintained that Jesus was just a smart guy who said a lot of wise things that we ought to follow. I did not see Him as anything more than a man. Perhaps a wise teacher who believed in the same God that I did, but certainly not the Son of God.

By the time I was a freshman in college, I was growing in my understanding of God and learning to feel God's presence, but I had yet to accept Jesus. I was able to worship God and thirst after God's wisdom and truth without seeing the role that Jesus played in the picture. Things went on like that for a number of months until one random Thursday night in February.

On that fateful night I was in the middle of singing worship songs with a group of my Bible Study friends on campus when it all just hit me. As we were singing songs about Jesus, I came face to face with the realization that He was telling the truth. I realized that Jesus was offering me a choice, and I could follow Him if I wanted to. I realized that there was some sort of decision to be made, and the option was sitting in my lap. I was standing at the fork in the road, and somehow, by some mystery, Jesus was there with me in the room. I could feel it. In that moment Jesus was offering me something I could not fully grasp, but some place deep in my heart responded to it. I said yes. And part of the mysterious invitation I sensed from Jesus was simply to take Him at His word.

I wanted to take Him for a wise teacher, not as the Son of God, but the problem is that's exactly who He said He was. He claimed He was sent from the Father, and we each have to decide for ourselves if we are going to believe Him. Taking Him at His word was fourth gear for me. That was a radical jump in my thinking.

Learning to see Jesus for who and what He claimed to be—instead of what culture, friends, media, or my own mind portrayed Him to be—was a gradual process. Once I said yes to Jesus, I was able to accept Him on His terms and start an authentic relationship with God.

Fourth Gear: *Jesus is who He claimed to be.*

The remarkable thing about Jesus is that if He were actually God's Son, it would add unprecedented value to the words He spoke. It would mean that Jesus is actually going to do what He promised—that one day He will return and set everything right. It would mean that your story is not over yet—that redemption is coming and the moment we accept this reality we shift into fifth gear.

As hard as it was to grasp the idea that Jesus is going to make a New Heavens and New Earth, I knew that if I was going to trust Jesus for *something*, I had to trust Him for *everything*. If I was going to trust Him for my forgiveness and salvation, I also had to trust Him to deliver on the future that He promised, and this fills us with a genuine sense of hope unmatched by the things of this world.

Fifth Gear: *Jesus will return to usher in a New Age and renew the entire Cosmos.*[13]

And that is how I came to faith in Jesus. This journey was not easy for me, and I stalled at a lot of intersections. I only learned how to shift from one gear to the next through trial, error, and painstaking difficulty. I had to build the plane while I was flying it. I only learned to drive the car after I purchased it, but I was determined to master the art.

I cannot tell you how many times I showed up to Tuesday night Bible Study and made a fool of myself. More than once I felt the burn of embarrassment in my cheeks as I tried to publicly figure out what on earth was going on. Sometimes it felt like stalling my car through an entire spiritual green light, as people honked impatiently behind me. It took a lot of humility and determination, but all along the way I was drawn by something bigger than myself.

My journey to faith was fueled by little glimpses of God, many of which came from the dozens of Christians I encountered over those critical years. They carried and reflected something I had never seen before. Something I wanted. And if there is only one thing I know about the Kingdom, it's that you have to want it.

---

[13] My little G20 only has five gears, so in her honor I will end the analogy here.

13 South America is real

Before I had any faith in God (when I was on the outside looking in) it did not make sense to me that in order to live a full life I would need to go into a building and have someone teach it to me. It made even less sense to me that I would need to join a club, small group, or religion. The very notion of it seemed odd. How could something be so essential to life but still be so concealed and hidden from view? The whole thing felt phony, because it seemed that life-altering truth should be more intuitive, and more accessible to the un-churched world. But over time I have come to discover and believe an important fact: if you pray and invite God into your life, and genuinely seek relationship with Him, things will start to happen. They might start happening slowly, and then just keep happening over time until the day you know through experience that atheism is impossible. That is a bright and glorious day.

One of the most outlandish claims of the Scriptures[14] is that when we seek God we will find Him. He says if we "knock at the door," the door will be opened. This is just about the boldest claim you could make about God. There seem to be a great many people in the world claiming they looked for God without finding Him. Most of these people conclude that God either that does not exist, or that He is completely detached and disinterested. As a result, lots of people find it really hard to understand the promise of seeking and finding, and most of us do not believe it.

I have wrestled with this promise myself, and I have had my doubts. But I think Jesus is saying that if we seek

---

[14] Aside from God claiming the title "Creator," and promising to remake and renew the entire universe . . .

God with our whole hearts and we are determined to head in the direction of God long enough, we will eventually encounter Him. In other words, Jesus is saying that if we head west long enough we are guaranteed to hit the Pacific. It is almost as if Jesus is reminding us that the Ocean of God is vast, immovable, and waiting for us, meaning that if you keep heading in the right direction long enough *you will collide with God.* Period. This assumes, of course, that you know which direction is west, and you have a compass to keep you on course.

Many of us do not know spiritual east from west, and many others do not have a compass to keep them on track,[15] but even assuming you *do* know which way is west, the whole quandary lies in the fact that you don't know how long it will take to get there. You may be headed west toward the ocean, but the catch is that in the moment you respond to the promise (spiritually speaking) you might be sitting in east L.A. or you might be in southern Illinois. We just don't know. In either case—if you head west long enough—the promise says that you *will* run into the Pacific. The principle still holds true, regardless of your starting point. The journey is longer for some than for others, but you can't miss it. If you seek it long enough, *you will find it.*

The catch is that we can't discern who is starting in Seattle and who is starting in Kentucky. Some of us start close, and we find God quickly. Others of us start far away and we should expect a long and difficulty journey. You may have to march across deserts of doubt, cut your

---

[15] In this case a compass would be the Scriptures or Jesus-centered community.

way through thick forests of assumptions, and push past endless rip-offs and shortcuts. You may have to forge rivers of uncertainty and scale mountains of resistance from friends and family, but if you truly want it and you persevere, there will be a day when you come stumbling out of the forest and onto the sand. One day you will reach the edge of the Pacific. On that beautiful day at the end of your long journey, you will sit at the edge of the ocean with the sun on your skin, soaking in the mystery. On that day you will be invited to sit at the edge of God's abundant love, and begin the redemptive process of renewing your heart and mind in light of the glory that lies in front of you. One day you will find what you were seeking.

But when we finally hit the Pacific, when we finally bump into what we were seeking after, it is not the end of our story but rather the beginning of the next chapter. Everything I have written of so far has been my journey to the Edge, and I have only begun to dip my toes in. Once we have arrived, whether we have walked from L.A. or Chicago, we sit at the edge of the ocean and in the healing presence of God we receive a whole new invitation.

If the first invitation is to seek the ocean and encounter it, then the second invitation is to explore the ocean itself. We are invited deeper into the mystery of God—to know Him and be known by Him. We are invited to explore the depths of His love, and the sheer variety and abundance of life contained in Him. You could spend the rest of your life exploring God and you would never exhaust the mystery. Just as you could spend the rest of your life exploring the Pacific and you would never be able to see it all. You could never capture it, know it, and understand it. It is simply too deep and too wide. There is too much variety and too many seasons. You would never be able to know every fish, rock, and underwater landscape, every tropical island and every glacial inland, every coral reef and every iceberg, let alone in each of their seasons and states. There is simply more there than you could ever explore and experience. So it is with the mystery of God.

God is deeper, wider, more mysterious, and more abundant than the Pacific, and our lives were designed to explore Him. We were created to integrate our hearts into His, moving toward an ever-growing knowledge of our Creator and Savoir.

We would be foolish to think that because we have bumped into the edge of the ocean, or even spent a few seasons on the high seas, that we have somehow arrived at some complete knowledge of the ocean.

Standing at the edge of the ocean face to face with the reality of God often raises more questions than it answers—lots more. I still have doubts and uncertainties. There are still so many things I do not understand. I still have yet to set foot on a thousand different tropical islands, let alone explore the depths beneath them. I have not seen enough to answer all my questions or erase all of my confusion. I cannot solve every tension, unravel every paradox, fill in every gap, or satisfy every question mark. But the longer I walk with God the more is revealed to me and the more real God becomes.

At some point, telling me God does not exist is like telling me that South America does not exist, or trying to convince me that the world is flat and has edges. I have never been to South America, so I cannot conclusively prove that it exists. I cannot even prove that the world is round, and I have traveled around it! But I believe these things on faith. I have heard about them and *seen their influence*. I believe that South America exists because I have heard stories about it and read books on it. I have met people who claim to be South American, and I see the ongoing influence of its culture and presence here in America. I have seen pictures of what I assumed was South America, and I have seen it drawn on maps. I have a firm idea of what South America is like in my mind, but I have never been there. Is it statistically possible that everyone agreed to trick me into believing that South America exists? Sure! I might be on the Truman Show. I have never set foot in South America, so I have to admit it is technically possible that it does not exist, but I believe on faith that it exists and the evidence weighs in favor of that faith. My belief makes sense with what I have seen of the world. The evidence of pictures, stories, and the pull of South America's cultural gravity and influence convince me that it is out there. Its culture, food, and people have impacted and touched my life, therefore I remain convinced that it exists.

The same thing is true of God and His Kingdom. I have read books about God and heard stories and *seen the influence* of that foreign Kingdom culture on my culture. I see evidence of His in-breaking Kingdom here and now, and I feel the pull of its gravity, but I have never been there. I have never seen God. I believe by faith that God exists, not unlike the way that I believe by faith that South America exists, and yet I would argue that my belief in God is even more justified because I can *feel* God. I have seen people healed by Him, but I have also been healed. He has spoken to people in my community, but I have also heard His voice. I have seen Him redeem hearts and minds from the inside out, but He is redeeming mine as well. His movements and love, His voice and healing, His redemption and presence can be *felt*.

Having spent most of my life being either atheist or agnostic, encountering God was shocking. It sent shivers down my spine and turned my little world upside down. For me, colliding with God was the equivalent of actively believing that South America did not exist, only to slam into it on my way from Spain to New Zealand. The atheist who runs into God is not unlike the early European explorers from my fifth-grade project. They are Columbus and his men, who set out across the Atlantic fully expecting to land the Indies. They believed that nothing but water lay in between them and that distant land, and they understood the basic principles of sailing, but as they crossed the Atlantic something unforeseen happened. They slammed into a new continent, and the discovery must have shocked them.

For me, the process of discovering God was exciting, but not easy. It felt like setting out across the Atlantic and launching across a great ocean of inquiry and exploration, all the while assuming I would land in safely in India. But something happened along the way, and I slammed into a new continent. Encountering God was like discovering a landmass that was not on the map. It was not supposed to be there. I left Spain fully expecting to hit India but there was something else in the way, something new and unexpected.

At that point I had two choices. First, I could pretend that I had in fact landed on the shores of India. I could live in complete denial. I could label the people I met "Indians" and attempt to explain everything else away. I could try to speak Hindi with them and attempt to buy spices and mangos, all the while ignoring the elephant in the room and the gravity of my misunderstanding. I could probably skate by operating under these assumptions. I could probably trade for *some* type of goods and bring them back to Spain. I could survive, and I would have my dearly held version of the story to tell when I arrived back in Spain, but in actuality I would have a very skewed view of reality.

On the other hand, I could accept the invitation and acknowledge the truth. I could summon all the courage and humility I had, pull out my pencil, and start redrawing the map. I could erase and redraw the lines, admitting that my best assumptions and clever guesses had been wrong, and acknowledging that I had just run into something mysterious and unforeseen.

Having redrawn my map, I might even be freed up to embrace and enjoy this new continent and the adventure it offered. I might be empowered to accept it with open arms and engage fully in its exploration and enjoyment. I could trade for valuable fur and gold, and I could return to Spain with a new map and a grand story to tell. I might even get a national holiday out of the deal. If only I could find the humility to say "wow, I had it all wrong," I would be freed up to engage in this new adventure.

Ironically enough, the very same options and invitations are extended to the atheist who lands on the shore of God's existence, and to any explorer who slams into this new continent. When we set out on a journey of spiritual exploration and collide with God, bumping into the edge of that mysterious territory, we have a choice to make.

Most of us sadly choose option one. We pretend that what we have landed in India. We pretend that our assumptions about the world remain correct and that everyone else must be wrong. We cling to our version of reality, labeling this new discovery an illusion, a myth, a dangerous tradition, or a random force in the universe. We attempt to explain away anything that does not match our current map of reality.

As a former atheist, I know how the thinking goes. We put labels on everything using physics and psychology and in our pride we think we know it. We think we have some unique right to proclaim what is and is not possible in the world. We set ourselves up to be the judges of what is true and false, of what can and cannot occur, all the while skating on the thin ice of mathematical logic and atheistic science.

To label something is not to own it, and the ability to observe physical phenomenon gives us no right to make spiritual and philosophical conclusions about life in the universe. Whenever we try to turn a limited set of physical observations into a life philosophy, religion, or anti-religion we end up with ideas that are flat and uninspiring. Jesus offers us living ideas, and we stay planted on them, energized by them, and passionate about them because there is One who exists behind them. He ignites our concepts and theology, energizing our whole body of thoughts about Him. We cannot easily change our minds and believe something else about the universe, because His love reverberates through our beliefs with such a beautiful depth and frequency that it rises up like a holy song, ringing with a sense of authenticity and truth.

Jesus' ideas are deep and multifaceted, and their depth exposes our alternative ethos as decidedly flat and one-dimensional. The logic and tidiness of the atheist doctrine—once so attractive to the mind seeking to stand on defensible truth—becomes the very quality that exposes its falsehood. For it sings no song, it speaks nothing to our souls. Atheism does not resound and resonate with the counter intuitive beauty and multifaceted grace that would actually account for the staggering splendor of creation, let alone the hopeless complexity of the human soul.

Somewhere deep in our psyche we intuitively sense there is something more, that atheism is too sterile to give birth to the world we know, but the atheist mindset feels safe and defensible. In fact, the illusion of defensibility may be atheism's most attractive quality. From our lofty fortified position we are free to launch an assault of skepticism, cynicism, and mockery upon any view or theory that might threaten our sense of safety; anything that threatens to push us off the rock of atheistic logic and into the waves of uncertainty below. But eventually we are confronted by unexpected encounters and just like the explorer who slams into a new continent, we have a choice to make.

On the one hand, we can choose ignore the elephant in the room and go around trying to buy spices and mangos in a world where it doesn't make any sense. We can stumble around trying to speak Hindi in a land that has never heard the language. We can close our eyes to what otherwise would be a new adventure and a fresh opportunity, opting instead to live in a false reality.

But those who thirst for adventure, who long for the frontier, and who have the humility to stomach true exploration, there is another way: we can choose to embrace the adventure with open arms, pull out our pencils, and blaze a new path. We can dive head first into the mystery, redrawing our maps as we go.

God says that if we seek Him with our whole hearts, we will find Him. He wants us to risk everything in order to hop on a wooden ship and start exploring the new world that is right at our fingertips. God says that if we live America and head west, we will hit the Pacific. He says if we leave Spain sailing for India, we are going to slam into something new and unexpected, and we need to be prepared to redraw the map when we do.

14 Resurrecting a Word

**The best journeys are not those in which
new lands grace our eyes, but those
in which we see the world through new
eyes altogether.**

I think most people in my generation assume that
following Jesus is about religion. They also assume
that religion is a really weird thing. I went to law school
at Lewis & Clark College in Portland, Oregon and most
people at Lewis & Clark tend to think that religion is a
strange thing. In 2009, the Princeton Review rated Lewis
& Clark "the most Godless school in America." I actually
love my school, and I love the people who go there, but the
culture is pretty resistant to the Gospel. When someone
starts talking about God or faith most people roll their
eyes or try to politely hide their disdain. I was not one to
talk openly or boldly about Jesus, and on more than one
occasion I had people tell me to "pass the Kool-Aid." I did
not blame them for it, because I was like that once, and I
did not get upset, because anger never changed anyone's
heart. For the most part I just tried to understand my
classmates and love them well, because they needed to
know that I cared long before they would listen.

As distant as many of my law school classmates were
from God, I think they were a fairly accurate reflection of
my city. Many of us in the Northwest carry around this
attitude that the unseen is unreal, and to operate off the
unseen is dangerous. We feel uncomfortable with religion,
and we get uneasy when people are passionate about
things that cannot be seen or scientifically proven. On top
of all that, I think the students at my school and maybe
young people everywhere have attached really negative

connotations to a lot of the words associated with Jesus. Take these words for example:

God. Church. The Bible. Pastors. Priests. Sermon. Christians. The New Testament. Evangelism. Repentance.

Feeling uneasy? For years these words made me shudder. Some of them still do. For many people, these words are associated more with uncomfortable confrontations, politically charged rallies, and awkward family dinners. Most of those words do not evoke any sense of peace, contentment, or intimacy with God. In todays culture many of us label religion as strange, superstitious, outdated, and naïve. We will come up with any excuse to keep our distance. Many of us do not want to acknowledge God, not because it is illogical to do so, but because the picture we are offered of God is just so unattractive.

Religious people can be crazy, judgmental, and even extreme. They told me I was going to hell. They make me cringe sometimes. They can be hypocritical, dry, dull, boring, close-minded, self-righteous, foreign, awkward, fundamentalist, and hyper-conservative. As a Christian, it is pretty unnerving to see the things that people do, say, predict, and broadcast in God's name. I see Christians all the time that do not reflect the God I know or embody what is actually written in the Bible.[16]

---

[16] In all fairness, I do dumb stuff too. I do things that are not reflective of my identity in Jesus or my future in His Kingdom. I can be unloving, ungrateful, and judgmental. The only difference is that it's easier to see other people's flaws than my own.

You could watch CNN for years and never come close to catching a real glimpse of who God is or how powerfully He can redeem. We just don't see the good stuff, which leaves a lot of room for us to confuse the good stuff and the bad stuff in our minds. We build walls out of our negative associations, distancing ourselves from God, and our hearts yearn for redemption, but what really needs redemption at the end of the day is the place those controversial words have in our hearts. Those words need to be resurrected—they need to take on new meaning and be seen through new eyes. Many Christians have failed miserably in representing Jesus to the world, *including me*. When we fail to feed the hungry and love our neighbors as ourselves, we fall short of His glory. When we judge and condemn and criticize each other we fail in representing the Prince of Peace and His Kingdom. When we fail in loving our enemies and those who belittle us we have failed to fully reflect the glory of God.

When we tell people that they are condemned to hell because they are not good enough instead of reminding them that God wants to save us out of the hell we cling to because He is really good, we can make the Gospel pretty awkward.

Some people claim to love God, but they hate others. Most of us can picture these people because they are the ones who make the news. They are the loudest and most visible among us. The Scriptures have a name for these people . . . they are called liars. The Bible says that you *cannot* love God and hate other people because the two are unavoidably connected. If you hate others, you are by definition not loving God because your will and God's will are not aligned. Yet every charge we have against the Church is based on acts in which people disobeyed God by hating when they were supposed to love. All of the hurtful and embarrassing acts carried out in the name of God are done in hate, instead of the selfless love that Paul begs us to embrace.

In my atheism, I thought hatred and turmoil were the results of religion. I thought that the concept of God corrupted people, but all too often it is people who have corrupted the concept of God. We create our own version of God, one who can sign off on the hatred we long to express, and the rest of humanity sits on the outside looking in and they are not inspired. As a younger man I was not convinced there was any truth in Christianity, because from the outside looking in I failed to separate human corruption and human institutions from the God who is real, humble, loving, infinite, personal, and passionate.

Most of us fail to separate religious people from the God they claim to follow, and as a result we brush aside religious rhetoric or tune it out altogether. Most of us have heard by now that the Bible says to love your neighbor as you love yourself. You have heard that God is love. You have heard that Jesus saves. *"Yeah, yeah,"* we think, *"I've heard that one before."* I don't doubt that you have, but have you ever *seen* it before? Stop and think. Most of us have not. Have you ever seen a world, nation, or even a neighborhood where people love God and always put others before themselves? I never have.

I think we underestimate the power and beauty of the things we read in the Bible because we have never seen them before. We fail to recognize how shocking they would be in action. We fail to grasp how refreshing and transformative it would be to live them out with the people around us. We can't even imagine a world in which everyone follows the Ten Commandments, let alone a world in which we are filled with the Spirit of God in order to finally accomplish the will of God. Don't assume you know what that world would look like. You are not living in a place where God's will is always done. Most of us live in a place where a frighteningly small amount of God's will is done. You may have heard a thing or two about the Kingdom of God, but we have not even scratched the surface of it yet.

So before you brush off all this fluffy rhetoric about loving your neighbor, think about what it would look like in action. Think of what it would *feel* like. Imagine if your enemies started loving you before they even learned how to like you. Imagine a world where the most popular and celebrated among us washed the dirt off the feet of the hurting. Imagine if people thought about your needs before their own, and no one ever starved to death. We have yet to see that world. Most of us have not stood in the presence of that much Grace. We have not tasted it yet, and in our own way I believe each of us is starving for it. We are all starving for the Kingdom of Heaven.

As for the few that have tasted it, they will never be content with a worldly lifestyle again. Individualism becomes stuffy and constricting, greed loses its appeal, and suddenly we no longer want to be the center of our own lives. When we get a taste of Kingdom culture, the words of the Bible come to life and take on irresistible appeal. Once you have been loved by your neighbor and loved him in return, "every man for himself" becomes a major letdown. Once you have felt the loving presence of God, the act of worshipping yourself is revealed as self-destructive.

The challenge is not simply teaching people who Jesus is on paper. The goal is not to memorize grace and forgiveness as definitions on a page, or teach the next generation how to pass a spiritual test, the goal is for them to live with the living Answer in their hearts, and in order for that to happen we need to rediscover the beauty of those old, worn out, religious words.

Sometimes it is those religious words (and not just the human soul) that longs for restoration. Those words long to be redeemed in our hearts, to be resurrected with a new and accurate beauty and meaning and significance. They long to dwell in our minds with all their intended depth, glory, and complexity.

When these words become dull recitations our hearts begin to starve. Our minds are left wanting and bored. The fire of our souls begins to die down and falter. You have heard these words of love and salvation spoken before, but have you ever seen them? The Scriptures say, "*Taste and see* that the Lord is good!"[17] Not "guess and pretend that God is good." Not "skate by and fake that He is good." *Taste* and *see*.

Before we set all these worn out words and concepts aside, before we scrap all that appears religious and dismiss it as outdated and unnecessary, stop and imagine what they would look like. You have heard those words before, but do you *know* them in your heart? You have heard about God before, but have you encountered Him yet? You may have heard of a homeless Galilean peasant

---

[17]   Psalm 34:8.

and His redemptive love, but have you been redeemed by it? When you do, there will be life in places you have only known death, and light in places you have only known darkness. Words like "salvation" and "love" will have a meaning beyond that which you have ever given them before. Those words will grow and stretch beyond the boundaries you have placed on them.

The goal is for us to know the depth of those words so truly and completely that we rejoice at the mention of grace, that we weep with joy when we are told we are forgiven, and our hair stands on end at the mention of our Savoir and the coming Kingdom. The goal is to know the depth of reality contained in those few simple words.

15 The Jesus Show

"I am the light of the world, all who follow me will not live in darkness, but have the light of life."

– Jesus[18]

Our greatest fear is not darkness, but light. This is the paradox of the human condition: we ask for light, we long for light, but we are terrified to enter in.

After I graduated from college I lived in the Greenlake neighborhood in Seattle, which is named after the lake situated at its center. The lake itself is unique from most of Seattle's lakes because the entire lake is a public park, encircled by multiple walking trails. Greenlake Park is the most popular park in Seattle, and in the summer months thousands of people show up daily from around the city to swim, bike, run, and play. My weekly bible study would gather there from time to time to sit in the sun and study the Scriptures together. I had been following Jesus for a few years, but I still had a lot of questions about my faith. In fact, I still had just as many questions as the day I gave my life to Jesus, the questions just changed over time.

During one our studies, as I sat at a picnic table and watched the constant stream of joggers circle the lake, it struck me that most of them probably did not know God (or believe that He existed to begin with) and yet I was

---

[18]   John 8:12

sitting right there studying the Scriptures, and God was so real to me. So I started complaining to my friends about God. *"I don't get His plan. I don't understand the method. Why so hands off? Why not just show up and start talking to us? Why is He so far away? How could so many people live out their entire lives and have no real idea that He's there?"* It just seemed too weird. My bible study friends normally had pretty good answers to my questions, and I would normally forget them within a day or two and go back to questioning things.

My friend David thought it was not a matter of how much God was revealing Himself. In his opinion, even if more were revealed, most people would still not believe and to a certain extent I believe him. Way back in the day there were people who stood toe to toe with Jesus, talking with Him face to face and watching Him perform miracles and they still did not believe. Some people saw Him murdered in public, and then they saw Him days later when He was alive again in a resurrected body, and still they doubted. Which leads me to believe that faith is not an issue of evidence. I think there is a certain type of evidence waiting for those who desire it, but I also think we need to live in the tension between doubt and faith. Even if we were given more evidence, many of us still would not find faith in our hearts. Some of us have unknowingly set an impossibly high standard of evidence as the threshold for our faith. Which begs the question: *what would prove to you that God exists?*

Seriously. Stop and think about it.

If Jesus appeared to you today, as He appeared to people two thousand years ago, would that actually build your faith? He did not have a halo. He was not popular among the powerful or the religious. He was not even particularly good looking. He was an average looking man with an average name, born to a teenage mom in a small town. When Jesus talked about faith, He just pointed us back to the Bible of all things.[19] He said that the Scriptures are strong enough to be the foundation for our faith. In other words, the Scriptures tell us everything that we really need to understand. They reveal a sufficient amount of information to cross the threshold into faith and satisfy our standard of evidence.

He said that if we cannot believe the Scriptures (and find God through them) then it would not matter if someone died, came back to life, and told us about their experience—it still would not be enough for us. In other words, if an honest examination of the Scriptures is unable to get us to a place of faith and trusting in God, we may be looking for the wrongs things in the wrong place. It might mean that our standard of evidence is set artificially high, and that even if we got the most obvious type of proof we could get (i.e. someone we know dying, seeing God, and then coming back to life to tell everyone) we still would not believe.

But Jesus did miracles, that would help, right? Well maybe . . . but maybe not. If Jesus showed up in person tomorrow afternoon and performed miracles on national television, most of us probably would not be moved to faith. Some would, but most of us would still have some excuse, some reason to doubt, some reason to ignore Him and go on worshipping ourselves. The miracles would

---

[19]   See Luke 16:31.

not be enough. We would just label Him as some sort of magician and then move on. I know that sounds harsh, but I think it's true. Personally, I would probably think it was a hoax, and in either case it would leave me feeling uncomfortable. Chances are I would shrug Him off and change the channel and I would not be alone.

But if that were true, it would mean that issues of evidence and complaints of God's proximity might not be as legitimate as we often play them up to be. It would mean that many of us—to varying degrees—have intentionally chosen spiritual blindness. We would rather close our eyes and make all manner of excuses, anything to keep our hearts from being confronted with the uncomfortable truth.

So the question remains: *if you could demand anything from God in order to prove that He exists, what would you want?* Would you want to hear God's voice? Perhaps have God appear as a brilliant ball of light in your room? What if God healed your sickness? What if God gave you the desires of your heart? What if God tore open the sky and struck down all the people who oppose you? What if He provided you with a high-paying job? Would that be enough? Maybe.

But I would argue that for *some* of us, *none* of these things would actually inspire genuine faith. They might help shake things up, they might get us to question more of our own assumptions, but if one of those events actually happened right now, would it really be enough? Probably not. After a miraculous recovery from cancer, the death of your enemies, or the second week at your new job, the excitement would wear off, and most of us would go back to living our normal lives. God could show himself as a brilliant ball of light in your room, but if your heart did not change then nothing else would change either. Even if our wish was granted, we still wouldn't come to faith. Which suggests that God's proximity is not actually what is keeping us from knowing Him. We are.

We have not been left in a world without evidence; it is not impossible to find proof. In fact, I think some of the best proof we have of God's existence is His Spirit, or what we commonly call the Holy Spirit. When it came time for Jesus to give His life for us, He told His disciples that the world would be better off if He physically left and sent God's Spirit instead. That is tough for most of us to grasp, because Jesus is saying that if we were given the choice between having Him here with us (as a physical person, in one location) *or* having His infinite Spirit meeting with billions of us simultaneously all over the planet, the Holy Spirit it the better choice. Most of us do not believe that, which means that either Jesus was lying or we have seriously underestimated the power and presence of the Holy Spirit in our lives.

Most of us would rather have Jesus here in person. Can you imagine how cool that would be? We could talk with Him and listen to His stories. We could ask Him questions and have a clear voice to answer us. We could even give Him a late night talk show and He could field calls from around the world, answering tough questions and encouraging people in their faith. He would probably end each show with a couple healings, or maybe even a resurrection. His ratings would go through the roof.

He could comment on politics and tell us who to vote for, give us killer investment tips, and then throw in some advice on how to deal with pesky neighbors. He would probably cast out demons and help people overcome alcoholism and selfishness. He would put Dr. Phil to shame.

He could tell us stories about the creation of the world, and what is inside black holes. He could tell us what the future will be like, and how He intends to rule and reign. He could share insight on life in the Kingdom and teach us how to prepare for it.

Or we could have the alternative.

We could have His Spirit simultaneously operating in and through billions of people all over the world: transforming hearts, redeeming lives, and restoring us to be more like God. The Holy Spirit could free people from alcoholism, selfishness, and physical ailments. God could speak to us directly, empowering us with words of love and affirmation. People all over the world (even people without cable) could hear from God, come alive to their destiny, and partner with God in the redemption of the world. The Holy Spirit could be physically and spiritually sustaining billions of people, dwelling in their hearts by faith and connecting them to the very heart of God. Jesus said this would be the better of the two choices, and right now as you read these words *that is exactly what is happening.* Welcome to reality.

We live in a beautiful world, but to be honest most days I would rather have Jesus here in flesh and blood. I get the feeling that most of us would rather tune in to His talk show then live the lives we have now. Which means that most of us (myself included) have severely underestimated the power and availability of God's Spirit in our lives. How else can you explain the fact that so many of us would choose the worse of the two options? I probably need to wake up to the fact that God is real, present, and accessible in my life right now, rather than sitting around wishing He would be more obvious about stuff.

If having your own personal burning bush or hearing the audible voice of God would not inspire true faith—if tuning in to "The Jesus Show" would not help you—it is probably because you are looking for God in the wrong places. God has revealed a lot about Himself and made Himself approachable and accessible, but we often struggle through our own spiritual confusion and darkness purely because we want God to jump through *our* hoops and perform for *us*. Perhaps if God did the impossible things that I want to see, in the time, place, and manner that I desire, then I could be persuaded to believe that God exists.

Think for a second about the seemingly impossible things that God has already done. Have you ever seen pictures of deep space? Or watched a perfect sunrise? Or looked into the eyes of someone God freed from addiction? Or wondered at how you were formed and created in the womb? Or seen uncontainable love bursting out of a redeemed human heart?

The question ultimately is not *"what would prove to me that God exists?"* That question holds value simply because it invites us to question our own attitudes and assumptions, but ultimately we should ask *"God, what is keeping me from knowing You?"*

I have a friend named Mark who grew up in the Church, and yet he never really believed or had a relationship with God. Eighteen years of church resulted in little to no faith. Even as Mark went off to college he had no genuine belief, until late one night in his dorm room. The pressure of his new circumstances had been mounting, until finally things came to a head, and for whatever reason, Mark got down on his knees and prayed, but this was not a pleasant prayer praising God for His greatness or glory. He was not thanking God for the things he had been given. He was angry. He prayed an honest, angry prayer at God, and for an entire hour in his dorm room he poured out everything that had been bothering him. He told God all the reasons he did not believe and all the problems he had with faith and religion, and he told God that he was *angry*. Then, at the end of that long prayer, he felt God speak to him for the first time in his life, and he heard a single word . . .

"Finally."

This was the moment that he started the process of giving his life to God and following Jesus. This was the moment he was actually able to start walking. We should never forget that God is bigger than anything we can put on Him, and that includes our anger, doubt, and fear. If you have doubts, voice them. If you have questions, ask them. If you have concerns, share them with someone you trust. Finding God is about stripping away the fake, it is about destroying falsehoods. It requires light, not darkness. It requires exposure, not secrecy. It requires honesty, not half-truths. Drag everything into the open. Be aggressive in your pursuit. If you are angry, pray an angry prayer. If you are doubting or confused or uncertain, you can talk to God about it. The key is to keep moving forward, and to search until you find.

God makes some bold claims about those who seek Him. Jesus says if you pray in His name (meaning in

His *nature*) for things in line with His heart—then your prayers will be answered. Through Jesus we enter a familial relationship with God as our Father and He loves giving good gifts to His children. This gives us the space, freedom, and permission we need to be really bold. Don't pray for a Porsche and then throw up your hands when you don't get one. Pray that you would know God and see Him at work. Pray that He would move in your heart and work redemption and restoration. Pray that God would bring His Kingdom in your life, *even if it makes you uncomfortable, even if it costs you something.* If God is an illusion, then what is the harm?

Looking back, I think that God responded to my friend's prayer because he was honest and he had passion. He was not trying to be religious or say the things he thought he was supposed to say. He was not dressing it up or hiding his true heart. I have a hunch that most of us are not totally honest in searching for God and that God craves the honesty we are so reluctant to give. And to be honest, I think some of aren't honest because we don't really want to find Him. We just want to be able to say that we tried so that we can have permission to go back to living our old lives. Too often we muster a half-hearted search, and what we need more than anything is to have genuine desire for God in the first place. We need to acknowledge our own thirst, and then be passionate in our pursuit. Generally speaking, we lack desire and passion.

Americans tend to rely on good hospitals, comfortable homes, fully stocked fridges, and large retirement accounts. In doing so we've convinced ourselves that we don't need God. Most of us don't feel a burning desire to seek Him. We aren't left with a lot of incentive to seek. We get pretty complacent in times of abundance, and it can pacify us if we let it. I think there have been entire seasons of my walk with Jesus where I was too crippled by comfort to actually seek God's will for my life.

Sometimes I wish we were in need of daily bread so that we would turn to God to provide it. But we have our bread and our Escalades and our Netflix, and therefore we fail to hunger for the greater gifts. In fact, I recently read a story about Socrates that I think is illustrative of our problem. In the story, a boy comes to Socrates to gain wisdom and understanding, and so Socrates takes him out to the ocean and leads the boy up to his neck in the waves. Then the old man grabs the boy and shoves his head under the water, as the boy struggles to reach the surface. Just before the boy drowns, Socrates releases him, and he chokes and coughs up water as he stumbles his way back to shore. Back on the beach, he angrily approaches Socrates for answers, and Socrates calmly asks the boy, *"What did you want most, when you were out there in the waves?"* The boy thinks for a moment before responding, *"I wanted air."* Socrates smiles back and replies, *"When you want wisdom as badly as you wanted that air, then you shall have it."*

I think the same is true of seeking God. We need to have that same passion. I think we need to crave God like we crave oxygen in our lungs. We need to have the courage and passion to seek after God with reckless determination. We need to set aside everything we think we know and seek after the Creator with genuine humility—because when we seek Him with our whole hearts, we will find Him. He is that good.

Regardless of your current understanding of God, I can safely say that you should expand it to include a concept of God that is more loving, infinite, present, relevant, caring, approachable, and forgiving than you or I think He is.

I once believed that people who had committed themselves to faith had become blind or oblivious, but I now I see that faith has not made me blind or oblivious, in fact it has done the opposite. I see all the things that I used to see in my educated atheism . . . and more. There is a difference between my worldview and that of the average atheist, and many of these differences are the direct result of our current faith systems, but now I know that these differences really stem not from a blindness caused by faith, but rather from what I had failed to see in my atheism. I used to look around and see a physical world of atoms and molecules—the slice of reality that we can detect through the organs we call eyes—and I accepted the small portion of reality they can actually perceive and said to myself, *"This is it. This is reality. This is all that exists. If I can't see it or explain it, there's a word for that, it's called imaginary. It must not be real. If my eyes cannot perceive it, it does not exist."*

I used to believe that, but now I know there is much more to reality than meets the eye. Our little organs can only pick up on so much of what exists, we can only grasp a fraction of the information available to us and only God knows what vast array of realities we fail to perceive. The Scriptures say that some of us will listen without understanding and look without grasping because we are stubborn and we have closed our eyes and ears. I think when we trust in God's version of the story we begin to perceive more of our reality, but the problem is that it takes an initial leap of faith to trust God in the first place.

There is a crazy paradox to understanding and perceiving God, a deep mystery that is difficult to articulate, a phenomenon that I cannot fully explain. We cannot fully understand Jesus (or the Scriptures) without the help of God's Spirit, but so often we do not invite God's Spirit into our hearts because we don't understand the Scriptures and what they say about Him. There is a tension between the two that must be overcome. We need God's assistance in order to fully understand the God whose assistance we need. Unfortunately, we often become stuck in the tension, fearful of moving forward without knowing more and unaware of the beauty that is waiting for us.

We are hesitant to truly invite God into our hearts, and yet once we do the Spirit empowers us to see God with such clarity that we are stunned that we did not encounter Him sooner, and we lament the fact that we waited so long to invite Him in in the first place.

Our understanding of God and the universe increases when we have God's Spirit living and breathing in us, and that only happens when we invite God's Spirit into our lives. Which really just means that in order to overcome the tension and experience God in our lives we have to *want it*. We have to seek Him recklessly and begin to exercise this little thing called "faith." We have to shake off our apathy and awaken our passion and desire, because if we learn how to crave God the way we crave oxygen, the whole world will begin to change.

16 Prison Break

"The Spirit of the Sovereign Lord is on me,
because the Lord has anointed me to
proclaim good news to the poor. He has
sent me to bind up the brokenhearted,
to proclaim freedom for the captives and
release from darkness for the prisoners."

— Isaiah 61:1

When I was a senior in high school, my friends Nick, Kristin and I decided to go on a road trip for Spring Break, so we started gathering for group meetings in Kristin's basement to scheme. We decided we wanted to do something big. We could not afford to fly anywhere, and there are only so many hours you can spend in a car together before your friends stop feeling like your friends. We figured after too many days we might start to lose our minds, or at least stop having fun, which limited our options even further. Sitting in Seattle, we pulled out a road map (those pre-iPhone paper ones) and convened our little council to address the most pressing question on a teenager's heart: what has more sun than Seattle and is really far from our parents? After a short debate we settled on the obvious choice . . . California.

We continued to meet in Kristin's basement weeks in advance to plan our trip—plotting the route and researching where we could camp along the way. We made our pack list, finalized our itinerary, created a budget, and then finally pitched the plan to my parents. We probably sounded like a few amateur entrepreneurs trying to find investors for our first venture. We presented our plan and waited in anticipation for the response. To our surprise, my parents not only said yes, they tossed us the keys to their brand new Ford Expedition and offered to buy us some food for the journey. I think I just stood there with my mouth hanging open. I hadn't expected our investors to actually buy the pitch, and I didn't know how to respond. To this day I am still impressed with my parents. I doubt I would give the keys to my new SUV to a couple of teenagers, but we weren't going to argue with them.

Two weeks later we piled our bags in the back of the Expedition and took off down the West Coast. Our goal was to follow the coastline to Monterrey, California, and then on to Big Sur. From Seattle we headed south on I-5 to Portland, Oregon before turning west toward the coast and Highway 101. After arriving at the Oregon coast we turned south again toward Monterrey Bay and the sunshine. That week was the first time I fell in love with the 101, because by the time you reach the Oregon coast it is more or less hundreds of miles of wild winding coastline . . . until you hit the Golden Gate Bridge.

For a couple of high school kids, it was the greatest adventure of our young lives. No parents, no rules, and no younger siblings—just a tank full of gas and the world at our finger tips. We journeyed down the coastline, camping as we went, and the further we traveled the more our anticipation began to build for San Francisco. We began to imagine what it would be like cross over that big red bridge and into the city, and the more we thought about it the more excited we became.

With our paper road map and Costco muffins in hand, we left Seattle under a thick cover of clouds. Gray clouds are nothing newsworthy for Seattle, but to our dismay the clouds followed us down the coast, and for days on end we ate, drove, hiked, and camped in the rain. The rain plagued us through Washington, through the entire state of Oregon, and right into the Golden State of California. We were four days in and we had not seen the sun, but it was going to take more than wet sleeping bags and a sunless road trip to dampen our spirits.

Our anticipation grew uninhibited as we approached San Francisco, and we charted our progress on our paper road map: five hundred miles, then three hundred, and then fifty. From fifty we probably counted down every mile in our enthusiasm . . . forty, thirty, ten, five . . . and then it happened. I will never forget turning that final corner, rounding that last bend in the highway, and seeing our bridge for the first time. It was towering and glorious—as impressive as it had been in our dreams.

To a few sixteen year-old kids the Golden Gate Bridge might as well have been the gates of heaven itself, and we were overcome by excitement as it came into view. We could not even allow ourselves to cross it without pulling off the highway and staring at it, as if we were paying it homage or something. We must have sat and stared at the bridge for nearly two hours before we were ready to cross it, enjoying the last of our Costco muffins and savoring the moment. To us, that bridge was more than a bridge, it was a symbol: it meant that we had succeeded. It meant that we had really left home and accomplished something. We had crossed our own little Atlantic Ocean and landed in a new world. We had arrived.

As we sat and stared out across San Francisco Bay, reveling in our success, the clouds that had plagued us from Seattle finally cracked and broke open. Sporadic beams of sunshine came pouring in, cutting through the gray clouds and lighting up the Golden Gate Bridge like stage lights from heaven. We soaked in every minute of it as our bridge glistened in the in-breaking sunshine, and the sound of gentle wind and distant traffic graced our ears. We could hardly contain ourselves, as our satisfaction spilled over into fits of joy.

After enough time had passed, we packed up our muffins and crossed triumphantly over the Golden Gate Bridge, buzzing with excitement as we surveyed our prize. By the time we crossed all four thousand two hundred feet of our red giant there was only one thing left on our San Francisco bucket list, and that was to visit the old island prison in San Francisco Bay known as Alcatraz. Alcatraz island was made famous by a number of things, including the imprisonment of Al Capone and the filming of several major motion pictures. But the prison doesn't house prisoners anymore and Hollywood stars rarely stop by to fight terrorists or film prison documentaries, so now people come by the boatload to see it.

From downtown we took a ferry out to the island for a day of exploring. Situated in the middle of the bay, the prison has some of the best views of the city, with bridges framing the San Francisco skyline and the bay at its feet. The ferry ride out and the view on arrival make the trip worthwhile, but the best thing about Alcatraz is the fact that you get to explore the remains of a high security prison.

Wandering through its halls and rooms, gates and cells, guard towers and walled courtyards, I was completely taken in by it. Wall after wall of stone, concrete, and barbed wire, all set against the best backdrop to ever grace a federal penitentiary. There is something gravely fascinating about prisons—something that captures our imaginations. There is something about standing in a place where so many people were incarcerated that impacts us. Sitting in one of the cells, I tried to imagine the people that lived out their lives there, and what it would be like to call that place home. I tried to imagine the sinking feeling that would set in as those heavy iron bars slammed shut, their infamous ring resounding off the concrete walls. I tried to imagine the way my heart would ache for freedom.

Standing there, with your hands on those cold iron bars, you cannot help but be moved by the place. Something draws a million people a year to visit the island—and I doubt it's just the view. It is ironic that the most exciting thing we could do with our free time—with our vacation time—was to a visit a prison. Why would so many of us use our liberty to visit a place that is antithetical to freedom? How could so many people from the "land of the free" spend time, money, and effort to see a place that was built to make people *not free.*

I think we have a dread fascination with prisons, in part because we hold our freedom in such high esteem. In the eyes of most Americans, and maybe most people, prison represents the ultimate punishment. For most of us, imprisonment is right up there with death and public speaking in terms of the worst things we could be forced to endure. We put such a high value on our liberty and freedom, that the containment of our bodies in prison is nearly synonymous (in our minds) with the death of the soul. Prison is slow-motion torture; it represents absolute depravity. We do not have the worst prisons in the world, but we do hold our perceived freedom in unusually high esteem. In our hyper-individualistic, independent, and liberty-driven culture, there are few things that are as repugnant as the idea of being imprisoned in a small cell.

Patrick Henry summed up the beating heart of America when he said, *"give me liberty . . . or give me death."* Our independence and free will are *sacred* to us. We believe they are pre-requisites to meaningful action, and that our physical freedom is necessary if we want to live anything close to a meaningful life.

The irony is that we are an imprisoned people.

As I walked the halls of Alcatraz, I was struck by the thought that most Americans spend vast amounts of our lives imprisoned by one thing or another. The only difference is that our prisons do not look like Alcatraz. They are not made of concrete and barbed wire, in fact the prisons we spend most of our time in are not physical prisons at all.

The very concept of a non-physical prison is a difficult one for us to grasp, (which is probably why we end up there so frequently) but the prisons I am referring to are not prisons for our physical bodies, they are prisons for the non-physical aspects of our personhood. It is fascinating how interwoven we are, how interconnected and fully integrated: we are body, heart, mind, and soul, all woven seamlessly together into a unique organism.

You are a holistic being and when one part of you becomes imprisoned, it affects all of you. Whether you recognize it or not (whether you believe that or not), you cannot imprison one aspect of who you are without infringing on the others. The imprisonment of the body certainly has an effect on your heart and mind, we understand that clearly enough, but the reverse is also true. The imprisonment of our hearts and minds affects our bodies. Take anxiety and depression for example, which are rooted in your heart and mind but take a devastating toll on your body. Or consider the fact that people can literally die of a broken heart. When we lose the will to live in our hearts and minds, our bodies fail soon after.

The irony is that for all the disdain we have for physical prisons, we are more than willing to accept the imprisonment of other aspects of our personhood. We rarely resist the imprisonment of our hearts, minds, and souls. But to understand how we become imprisoned, we have to start by building a basic understanding of that strange religious word called "sin."

Sin is a loaded word that frustrates most of us. It comes with a lot of baggage. Most of us do not clearly grasp it because we fail to grasp what the Bible says about the reality we live in. Sin forms the bars of our invisible prison cells, ruling and directing many of us, and yet our collective and cultural awareness of it is quite poor. What I want to say next is controversial. I know it will be confusing to some, and I approach it cautiously, but it must be said. The Bible describes our world as being a world at war. It claims that there is a struggle unfolding between the Kingdom of Light and the dominion of darkness. It claims there are angelic or spiritual beings, with real power and authority, on both sides of this battle and that human beings are caught in the middle. It claims that those who sit under the authority of the "ruler of this world" sit in the dominion of darkness, and it claims they are imprisoned— enslaved by darkness and enslaved by *sin*.

If you only understand one thing about imprisonment and sin, understand this: we were *born* into a corrupted world that has rejected God's light and by abusing its collective autonomy and free will, it has embraced the darkness, confusion, and foolishness that exist outside of the light. We were born into a frustrated and tense reality; a world where God's will is *not* always done. A world under the influence and reign of darkness; a world in which our hearts are bent toward self-worship. This forms the basis and foundation of our prisons. This sets the stage for an incarceration that we cannot see, smell, or touch.

So we have sin corrupting on one side, and the powers of darkness oppressing and misleading on the other, and the two work in tandem to imprison us. There is a symbiotic relationship between sin and the dark forces of this world. I am well aware that it is unpopular to talk about the demonic in our modern age, but Jesus talked about it all the time, and if we are to take Jesus seriously, we absolutely must acknowledge them. Often dark forces play the role of prison guard, working to keep us right where we are, attempting to foil our escape attempts. It turns out this spiritual battle is unfolding right on our doorstep, in our living rooms and classrooms, even in our minds.

In our modern skepticism we scoff at this stuff. We think the idea of demons or dark spiritual powers is the stuff of Hollywood movies and outdated myths. In our twenty first century scientific culture, with its anti-religious undertones, the momentum of our collective cynicism makes it difficult for us to acknowledge anything that sounds so ridiculous. Yet we cannot take Jesus at His word without acknowledging that we were born into this reality, where imprisonment through sin is natural and perhaps even the norm, and prison life is the default human experience that we must choose to depart from.

The irony of it all is that the most skeptical among us, those who are the quickest to deny the existence of spiritual imprisonment, those who are most likely to mock the idea of the kingdom of darkness or the power of sin, are tragically the ones who are most likely to be imprisoned by them.

But whether we acknowledge them or not, if we assume for the moment that dark powers and sin do in fact imprison us, it becomes critically important to grasp what sin is and *how* it imprisons us. This starts, I believe, by questioning our own concept of sin. We typically think of sin as a defined wrongful act—like violating one of the Ten Commandments, arriving at church mid-sermon, or sending a letter without the proper postage. We typically think of sin as either something you go out of your way to *do* or some strange religious infringement, but I think sin is far more comprehensive and ubiquitous. Sin occurs *whenever we are operating outside of the heavenly rhythms that God intended for us from the beginning of time.* If all you ever did was sit on your couch, watch movies, and "look out for number one," you would be living completely outside of the compelling vision God designed for human life, and that is sinful. In fact, in todays world I would argue that our rampant apathy and self-worship are bigger problems than any overt sinful act. Our indifference breeds more problems than any other sin, and indifference is outside of God's heavenly rhythms.

If you will accept this broad and sweeping definition of sin, the implication is that we are truly sinful from birth, because we are born with the inclination to be our own gods and operate outside of God's redemptive plan for the universe. The more we see of the Kingdom of God and its glory, the more obvious it becomes. *We fall far short of the glory of God and the love of His Son.* We do not have to see much of God's grace and character before this becomes abundantly clear by way of comparison. Our brokenness is most visible in the light of His wholeness— our corruptedness is highlighted by His perfection. The more we see of Him, the more we grasp the desperate nature of our own condition.

We were born into a condition of not knowing Him and not *belonging* to Him, and as we operate outside of God's heavenly rhythms, and outside of His Light, we are both operating in sin *and* we are left vulnerable to even greater sin and darkness. Which means that darkness can almost effortlessly gain a foothold in our lives. This darkness takes many forms, but it all has the same imprisoning effect.

The most obvious forms of imprisonment are addictions that we can diagnose: alcoholism, drug addictions, addictions to pornography and gambling. Those are real and imprisoning, but the majority of us regularly suffer from much more subtle vices. As a result, we fail to diagnose our sin and fail to see how it imprisons us. We fail to see how our brokenness keeps us from living in the hope-filled life-giving rhythms that God intended and how sin keeps our souls from soaring in unadulterated love.

We fail to diagnose that we are imprisoned by greed— that ever-increasing desire that always demands more and repels our satisfaction. Greed is the itch we can never scratch; the thirst that drives us mad by our inability to quench it. Greed compels us to cut corners, cheat, lie, clear-cut, and compromise with no thought of the consequences. Yet after we have taken advantage of our friends, our neighbors, and the planet, we still feel empty.

How many of us are slaves to our wealth? How many of us are *controlled* by what we already own, while simultaneously working ourselves to the bone in an effort to expand our little empires, ever fearful that we might lose what we have gathered? We tie our self-worth to our assets, and simultaneously elevate the importance of our wealth over the wellbeing of our friends. How often do we forsake happiness until we have more than those around us? How many of us have ruined friendships and alienated others with our stinginess? How many of us have failed to help those in need because we believe *"what's mine is mine"*? We cling ever tighter to our possessions as loneliness and isolation creep ever closer.

We fail to recognize when we are slaves to our own reputations and the expectations we perceive others have placed on us. How many of us are slaves to *their* collective wills and afraid to show our true selves, afraid to reveal our flaws; deeply fearing rejection? We put on the mask the world asks us to wear and then we trudge through life, ever diligent in upholding the image, maintaining the persona, and concealing what lies beneath it.

How many of us are imprisoned by hopelessness, with no enduring or authentic reason to feel joy? We find some shallow and fleeting thing to put our hope in, some future plan, some new friendship or romance, some new gadget to acquire, some new promotion to attain. We find a carrot to chase, one that will keep us distracted and provide some vague sense of hope and excitement; all the while wondering (if we even dare to wonder) what on earth we are really here for. We are a people who suffer from chronic and persistent hopelessness.

How many of us are slaves to our own corrupted desires, being led through life under the control of what we desperately hope will bring us happiness? How many of us believe we are free when in reality we are chained to our wandering urges and fruitless pursuits? How many of us believe that our next purchase, our next drunken party, or our next sexual adventure will bring us satisfaction?

How many of us are imprisoned by a lack of purpose? Running through life perpetually unsatisfied, restless to the core, relentlessly seeking but never finding, always chasing but never seizing? How many of us have resigned to believing that our only purpose in life is to scratch the itches that we were never intended to have in the first place?

How many of us are imprisoned by worry and anxiety, mulling over our endless fears, allowing our racing thoughts to steal our sleep and consume us? How many of us believe that our survival hangs on our shoulders and then devote our thoughts to inventing and imagining a thousand ways it could all go wrong? Our nerves are shot and peace feels a million miles away, but still we press on. Weariness and depression run rampant, fueled by our anxiety and nursed by our worried thoughts.

How many of us are imprisoned by our shame and fear? How many of us hide our feelings of inadequacy, suffering through circular cycles of denial, justification, and self-rejection? How many of us are imprisoned and controlled by that nagging and demonic voice that tells us we are not lovable, that we are not worthy, but that we should spend the rest of our lives trying to prove otherwise?

How many of us are imprisoned by unforgiveness and bitterness? How many of our days have been poisoned by hate and judgment? How many days have we allowed envy or jealously to rot our bones and steal our joy? How long have we been imprisoned by pride, proclaiming we know best as we drown in our unbelief and misunderstanding?

How many of us are slaves to religion? Believing that our good deeds and morality will earn us the love and approval we seek. We believe that our goodness will lift us closer to God and so we scramble along on the hamster wheel of religiosity, sometimes exerting incredible effort in hopes that God and others will see how good we are and reward us for it. We think we are headed somewhere but there we sit spinning in place. Our hearts are often far from God and we slip more easily toward judgment and self-righteousness than genuine love. We check all the right boxes, but we are a long way from tasting the richness of life that God intended.

How many of us are imprisoned by lust? How many are unable to truly see others as beautiful and fearfully made human beings, instead of objects of our fantasy? Sex and pornography rule over us like a slave-master, always demanding a greater sacrifice, always pushing us further, and never truly satisfying. They drive us to abandon relationships and sacrifice marriages, dragging us into lives of shame and secrecy and forcing us down roads where joy and innocence are crushed and left for dead. We sit imprisoned, unable to break the cycles of addiction, sacrifice, and desperation. Every sexual experience gives us a brief feeling of victory and so we orient our lives around finding the next fix, desperate to taste victory one more time but all along we are enslaved. We are being led deeper into bondage where true pleasure and flourishing sexuality are desperately out of reach.

We live in a nation of slaves who tell us they are free.

We place our hands on these cold iron bars of greed, reputation, un-forgiveness, anxiety, apathy, and religion. We are stuck in our cells of hopelessness, judgment, fear, and worry. We are stuck in our pride and misunderstanding, as despair and loneliness grasp at the edge of our minds. In reality, if we are being introspective and honest, most of us are not free.

Sometimes we recognize our prisons, but often we are blind to them. Sometimes we sense what sin has cost us something, but more often we keep chugging along. Most of us are content being right where we are (whether free or imprisoned) because the place we are is the place we *know*, and the unknown that lies beyond is a source of fear all its own. We feel safe in our prison cells, and just like Alcatraz, the view is often fantastic. Plenty of us have good-looking homes, good-looking families, and good-looking cars. Life *looks* good and the view is awesome but deep down we are still stuck, our bitterness festers, our broken desires hollow us out, our hopelessness and despair weigh us down; our wings are clipped, we are crushed, we are shackled. This is what sin does to us. It strands us, imprisons us, hollows us out, and weighs us down.

The fascinating thing about this spiritual, mental, and emotional imprisonment is that we so often fail to diagnose it, and as a result we look out on our good looking world and conclude there is no consequence for our sin. If we violate the rules of our government our punishment is a physical prison, but sin is different. When we violate the natural laws and rhythms that God purposed from the beginning of time *our very departure* from His presence is punishment within itself, because the departure is what imprisons us. The further we are from the Light, the more deeply encased we are in darkness, and if the crime is trespassing into darkness, then the crime is also the punishment. *Sin is punishment for sin.*

Please understand, this doesn't mean that violating God's way of life doesn't create fallout. Sin might not be the *only* punishment for sin. Most sin is accompanied by other natural consequences. There is a ripple effect, and sin often echoes into the future and costs us something. I am not claiming that you won't have to deal with a broken heart, broken friendships, depression, anxiety, hopelessness or any number of other natural and unfavorable results, because the fallout is real.

I am not promising there won't be any punishment either, or that God will never overtly enact justice, but the point is that even if there was no fallout or natural consequences—even if God never rebuked, punished, or intervened—*there would still be punishment inflicted* because the further we drift from the Light the more imprisoned we become. You need only to think about how sin twists our hearts and clouds God's nearness in order to sense the connection between sin and imprisonment.

The highest punishment is ultimately to be separated from God and left to our own devices. It is to live a life (and perhaps an eternity) increasingly departing from God's presence, until only a dark and empty void is left where a full heart was meant to dwell. In this growing depravity, we could simply be abandoned to endure ourselves forever and it would be a perfect hell.

We think God is a stickler waiting around to punish us for the all the "fun" we are having as we enjoy our "freedom," but what if God only wanted to show us a way out of our sin because to leave us in prison would be unloving and God is love? What if the natural effect of sin was to splinter, fracture, frustrate, degrade, and destroy the heart that embraces it, and God's unrelenting desire was to see those hearts set free and one day resurrected?

That would be awesome.

We tend to assume that Jesus was a tame guy with great table manners. He was probably great with kids and was easy to hang out with. According to all the pictures we paint He has a thing for lambs and He looks great on stained glass windows. It is easy to assume that He was a soft-spoken religious man who tucked His shirt in and followed all the rules, but I think He was more radical than we give Him credit for. I think He lived and died to challenge everything we know. He came to flip the theological, social, and cultural order on its head, and create a new order; one characterized by freedom instead of fear, by courage instead of imprisonment.

God loves us too much to watch us sit in prison. Sin, brokenness, and imprisonment are all abhorrent to God. Our Father wants more for us, so He made a way for you to be free. He sent Jesus to do something remarkable for us. It was in Jesus that our freedom was won. He took all the sin of the world, the very heart of our darkness and brokenness into His own body. All of it was laid on Him and He had to bear the weight of it, to feel the heaviness of it and perhaps even feel the shame and defilement of it. Then, after taking it all on his shoulders, He went to

His death where sin was nailed to the cross along with its bearer. Sin was put to death along with Jesus. He breathed his last and was laid in a tomb, but three days later the tomb was empty and the message was clear: sin had been defeated; death itself had been beaten.

To extend the prison analogy, something was accomplished in the death, burial, and resurrection of Jesus that directly affects our imprisonment. His sacrificial death on the cross painstakingly earned you a "get out of jail free card." As ridiculous and cliché as that may sound, there is a strange element of truth to it. I still cannot fully understand what Jesus did and how it all works, but somehow it does. I benefit from it, I experience it, and yet I do not fully understand it. I cannot comprehend the science or logic of it all, I cannot even grasp the power of love that would drive such an act. I am left clutching at the mystery of a God I cannot see or touch. Yet God rescues us, the prisoners who seek Him find Him, and I have watched Him set people free. Through the death of Jesus we gain the ability to re-enter God's presence, to step freely back into the Light, and no power of darkness can stand in the light. Jesus is greater than your vices, habits, or demons, and His heart is to set you free.

As Jesus walks through the prison, He knows the name and story of every prisoner and every single one is important to Him. He knows all our darkness and sin, and yet He loves us without doubt or reservation. This is redemptive love come among us in bodily form, but as He walks through our spiritual Alcatraz, most prisoners have a reason to ignore Him. After all, physical prisons are not all bad and even penitentiaries have their perks. Even prisoners get three square meals and a bed, and depending on the prison you might get Internet and cable TV. Prison might even be fun from time to time, and I imagine that most people settle in to some level of comfort there.

The same is true of our spiritual prisons, because sin can be fun too, and it has its perks. Dark powers have something to offer those under their control. If there were no perks to sin and darkness, if dark powers offered *nothing* but disappointment, then people would not spend their lives in sin. There are perks to being enslaved by wealth, un-forgiveness, and unbelief. Sometimes it just feels easier to live that way. Imprisonment aligns more easily with the natural flow of our corrupted hearts and our fallen world. There is a familiar ease to it and most of us settle into some level of comfort, forgetting there is a better way to live.

Being enslaved by sin can be fun, but just like sitting in minimum-security prison, the experience loses its appeal over time. Prison is not a fun place to be for any meaningful length of time. Eventually the novelty wears off and we find ourselves in a hopeless place where despair comes easy and genuine hope is almost impossible—a place where ever-increasing costs yield ever-decreasing benefits—where it takes more and more sin to feel waning hints of pleasure. We are hollowed out by a cyclical and enslaving pattern of existence.

Many of us find ourselves imprisoned and settle in for the long haul, resigning ourselves to the stuffy cell we stumbled into. We accept our limits, and we accept the fact that we may be there forever, because while our cells may not be comfortable they are *known*. And here is the catch: we are constantly willing to settle for the familiar and constricting over the liberating and unknown.

Some of us have been imprisoned since birth and we feel comfortable there. Some of us have no idea what lies beyond our cells, and others have been imprisoned so long they have simply forgotten. If a bird is caged long enough, he may forget he was meant to fly, and this creates all sorts of problems. No one attempts to escape to a place they are not aware of. No one yearns for a land they have forgotten, or longs to fly when they are unaware of their wings.

We can easily find ourselves stuck in sin, anger, discontentment, fear, bitterness, addiction, or hopelessness so long enough that we forget there is anything else. Prison becomes normative, and we accept our imprisoned place in the world. We are hardly even aware of the world that exists outside our prison walls, and so we settle into the comfort of the familiar, and the effects are devastating.

Studies have been conducted on inmates who served sentences of solitary confinement, which involves twenty-three hour lock down in a concrete cell. It is the worst type of imprisonment. The inmates start by hating those walls, and they nearly go insane trapped in that place, mentally tortured and powerless to escape. But after enough time they experience a mental break down before finally settling in and accepting their surroundings. It sounds like hell on earth, but studies found that years later, when they were finally released from prison, a curious thing happened: *the inmates recreated their cells.* They actually build cell-like environments in their homes, because the cell was all they knew. It is what they had become accustomed to and it felt *safe.* Was it pleasant? Absolutely not, but that dark place offered something *familiar* and comfortable.

When Jesus walks through our spiritual prisons, half the inmates turn their backs on Him simply because what He offers is something new, different, and unknown. We would rather sit in darkness than risk something on God and the life He offers. I think deep down we are actually afraid of such radical freedom. We are afraid of what would happen to us if we lived that far out on the edge, under the rule and reign of such abundant grace. Some of us are just afraid of our own potential, and we would rather cling to the familiar than dare to risk what we might be capable of in God's Light. But not everyone turns his or her back out of fear.

Some people are so dependent on the prison of sin—so addicted to it—that they don't want out to begin with. You might embrace darkness for its benefits, but the problem is that if you live in darkness long enough, you begin to develop a distrust of the light. You no longer believe the world outside of your cell is a safe place, and you begin to fear the very place you were designed to live.

For others of us it is not the comfort of our cell that holds us back, or fear of the unknown, but just a blatant pride. We long to get out of prison but we refuse to accept help. We are too proud to accept the grace that God offers and we would prefer trying to earn our own freedom. We recognize that we need saving, but we would rather save ourselves. When Jesus walks by their cells they snarl and turn up their noses *"I don't need Him, I don't need anyone. I can do this myself. If I got into this mess alone, I can get myself out."* We are stuck seeing ourselves as the center of our own lives, and as a result we believe *we* are the answer to the difficult questions posed by our imprisonment. Fortunately for us, although the answer begins with you, and begins with choice, *you are not the answer.* Pride and arrogance may be the worst of all human conditions for this very reason: they blind us to the Living Answer.

Pride keeps us from admitting our faults, which in turn keeps us from coming to Jesus. We stubbornly cling to our own little perspective, refusing to change our life maps. Not because our life maps are accurate—our hesitancy is not based on a search for objective truth—deep down it is a matter of safety. We are afraid to acknowledge God, because we are scared to abandon the perspective that has given us comfort, security, and a sense of normalcy, even if it imprisons us in the process. Abandoning our perspective would leave us vulnerable, and we will avoid that feeling of vulnerability at all costs, even if we harm ourselves in the process.

Take a hermit crab for example. They live out their lives inside the discarded shells of snails. As they grow up, they need to find new and bigger shells on a regular basis, but the moment they move from one shell to another is vulnerable one, because in that moment they are exposed to the elements and open to attack. It is a nerve-racking event, but the switch must occur once they have outgrown their shells. A hermit crab never desires to change shells, because the process leaves it vulnerable, but the same is true of our life maps and us. We never naturally desire to abandon one set of beliefs for another, but this creates a dilemma, because we will either die in our cramped little outgrown perspectives (in our undersized shells, imprisoned by our pride) or we must risk being vulnerable in order to find something more suiting, something that more accurately reflects our reality, something that gives us freedom and room to breath.

The problem is that we so often get confused about where freedom is found, and as a result we choose to sit in our cells. And as we sit in prison, the brainwashing begins, and the powers of darkness begin to speak lies over our cramped little shells. They tell us we are superior to everyone else; open minded and intellectual. They tell us we are free, and that we are better off in our damp little cells than the confusing world outside of them. If we don't know any better, we buy the lies. We actually begin to believe we are free, but we have to recognize and admit that we are in prison before we can desire true freedom. We have to recognize that we are wounded before we can seek healing. We have to wake up to the fact that something deep in our souls longs for God before we come to Him for sustenance. We need to admit that we are depraved and malnourished when we try to sustain ourselves on anything less. This is why humility is among the most beautiful qualities that we can pursue, because the sin that flows out of our brokenness will only find true healing in one place. True hope finds its source in one God.

Our hope has to come from something outside of our prison cells. You simply cannot generate lasting hope within yourself. It is unnatural, and we were never intended to apart from Jesus. In fact, I would argue we cannot even know *who we are* apart from Jesus, because we do not fully know ourselves (and what we are capable of) until we know that we are unconditionally loved. Love and grace draw something out from deep inside of us that we are not even aware of until they emerge. You cannot know the riches buried inside of you while staring through prison bars. Humility sets us free.

I used to think that in order to be humble I needed to have a low view of myself. I figured that if I always thought really low of myself, and refused to admit that I was good at anything, there would be no room for pride. I truly misunderstood humility, because while self-deprecation keeps you from being bigheaded, it also leaves no room for confidence, courage, or any number of other good and noble things that God desires in us. Humility is not thinking lowly of yourself, *humility is knowing exactly who you are.* Humility is being aware of both aspects of who you are in Jesus. It means you are aware that you are not a perfect little snowflake who deserves the attention and worship of those around you. You refuse to waste time trying to convince others that you are better than you really are (or that you are better than they are). You admit you are not the center of the universe, and that you are more imprisoned, broken, and sinful than you were ever prepared to acknowledge.

But on the flip side it means you are also willing see yourself the way that God sees you in Jesus. You are His child. You are holy, blameless, and pure. Through Jesus you are an adopted son or daughter who is reconciled, redeemed, and forgiven. You have tremendous value in His eyes, and you are loved more deeply than you would even dare to admit. These things are true even on the days you do not claim them for yourself, on the days you fail to walk in it—on the days you fail to act like it. These things are true even on the days you do not feel worthy of it.

God gives us a new identity in Jesus, one that breaks the cycle of self-imprisonment, because sin is (in part) a matter of who you believe yourself to be. God calls you His beloved. Your new identity is *son* or *daughter.* You are justified and forgiven, and when we claim that forgiveness for ourselves the Holy Spirit collides with our rusted worn out DNA and something brand new is born. You become nothing short of a new creation. From that moment on, God says you are a saint and it is not false encouragement or flattery. When God claims you and names you He is drawing out the truth, and that truth empowers us to break the cycle of imprisonment that haunts humanity.

As God renews our identity and breaks our chains, He also gives us the Holy Spirit, who dwells among us and *inside us*, and where the Spirit of God is there is freedom. All who belong to Jesus and walk with Him have the Holy Spirit inside of them, and when you live by the Spirit you live in love and walk in freedom.

If you do not belong to Jesus, you wander from one prison to the next. You are an old creation, and the laws of sin and death rule over you. That means you will naturally live a life of bondage and idolatry, and walk a path that inherently leads to death. The spirit of death that naturally flows out of sin deadens the heart and mind. We are left calloused and hard-hearted—devoid of any lasting hope or joy—and all of it leads quite naturally to spiritual, emotional, and physical death. Some of us sense this intuitively, and others deny it until the day we die. Some of us are convinced that this all just religious propaganda, or a fear tactic intended to pressure conversion, and there is nothing I could say to convince them otherwise. What would *you* say to someone who was imprisoned and did not know it? How would you describe sight to someone born blind? Where does one find words to overcome such relentless cynicism? What words could lead the hardened heart toward humility?

In the absence of such words, our spiritual prisons are bursting at the seams. Some prisoners are too arrogant to ask for help, some are too afraid to leave the safety of their cells, and others are simply oblivious to their own imprisonment, but God cannot stand to see you imprisoned. God's heart is to rescue and redeem, and He will slide a letter under your cell door to inspire you and give you hope, but He will also kick down the door and bust you out of there if you are willing to call on Him. He sent His only Son to carry out His will and reflect His character to our hurting world and what is God's will? *To set the captive free.*

Jesus approaches each one of us gently; ready to take the veil from our eyes and the chains from our hands and feet. He is eager to set us free. It is in arrogance that we believe we are not incarcerated, but humility rooted in faith enables us to receive what will make us truly whole.

If it is sin that imprisons us, then faith becomes the conduit through which cell doors are ripped open, because God's deepest desire in that moment is to flood your prison cell with light. Sometimes we get this idea in our heads that God wants us to be stuck in our prisons and suffer punishment for what we have done, but nothing could be further from the truth. God is more radical than that, and His grace is more redemptive than we think. God does not want you to sit in the darkness and "serve your sentence." God wants a prison break.

If you have never tasted God's freedom, if you cannot even picture what lies beyond your prison, if you have no idea what glory waits for you beyond the walls of your little "self-life," it will be hard to thirst for that freedom, but you have to learn to visualize that place even if you have not been there. Learn to imagine it in your mind and set your heart on it. We must be a people who thirst for something more, who hunger for lands we have yet to see. We must develop a taste for the Kingdom of Heaven, even though we have never been there and have only experienced the smallest glimpses of it by faith.

Jesus wants you to have life that is *truly* life, and there is joy waiting on the other side of that prison door. When we call out in Jesus' name, claiming His authority and admitting our need to Him, He begins the mighty work of swinging that prison door open, allowing us to walk out into a new world. Why? The simple answer is that God is good. The more complex answer is that Jesus was given all authority on heaven and earth, which means that He has power over sin itself and all the forces of darkness and depravity that imprison us. What did Jesus do with all that authority He was given? He humbled himself to the point of death, even death on a cross, and He made a way for God to share His authority (and His Spirit) with you. If you belong to Jesus, you share that power now. In Him you have power over anything that might seek to imprison you, because His Spirit dwells in you.

The key to unlocking this newfound freedom is choice. It starts with turning from our old worn-out ways and turning back to Him. This turning back, or "re-turning," is known as repentance. Repentance is another one of those religious words that comes with a lot of baggage, but the essence of repentance is simply *renewal*. Repentance is about renewing your mind. If we ever want to experience vibrancy and abundance we have to turn away from our cramped, futile ways of living, and turn our hearts away from the things that imprison us. Repentance and humility are the foundation for freedom and pre-requisites to spiritual exploration, and they are necessary if we are ever going to embrace the frontier.

You cannot live out the adventure that God has for you if you are bound and gagged in a prison cell. That is simply not how the spiritual life works. As human beings we are sheer potential. We are made in God's image, built with the capacity to embrace eternity, and yet our tendency is to chronically limit ourselves. We consistently come up with assumptions, rules, and boundaries that limit what we are capable of. I think Jesus lived out on the edge of what we believed was possible to show us that there are no limits. Jesus opened up a new frontier, and in doing so He demonstrated that God has no bounds. We have permission to throw out the rules. Boundaries of race, class, and nationality are useless and constricting. The laws of nature, which govern the wind and waves, are subject to His hand. The rules governing entropy, disease, blindness, and death can themselves be bent and broken. With God's Spirit, anything is possible. None of the prisons we find ourselves in are permanent or unshakable. There is not a door that cannot be pulled from its hinges. Sometimes we label our broken condition permanent and we believe ourselves to be beyond redemption, but in God's Kingdom *unredeemable is a myth*.

In my atheism I thought that faith blinded people, but faith is not about blinding yourself to anything. Faith is not about becoming dogmatic, hypocritical, or even moral. Faith is about *seeing beyond the boundaries*. Faith is about waking up to the staggering potential that exists in our Creator.

The Creator God entered into humanity to expose the fact that our world is not enhanced by the systems, borders, and boundaries we create—nor by the self-centered assumptions we build our lives on—but rather our world is diminished by them. Jesus came so that in the wake of His resurrection we could live lives that are fully integrated with God's Spirit, a life that is never permanently shackled or irreversibly derailed by sin and brokenness. Jesus showed us how tragic it is to be enslaved by things like money, lust, and religion, and He offers us more than a "get out of hell free" card. He offers more than a free pass to sin and do what we think will bring us the most pleasure in our own eyes. The mind-blowing opportunity that Jesus offers is to walk with Him in order to experience life to the fullest.

His vision for you is vibrancy; that you would wake up each day and accept His invitation to engage in the adventure that is right in front of you. His adventure is richer and more real than anything MTV or Hollywood offers us, and His invitation does not sound like any invitation you have ever received. Jesus invites you to die to yourself so that you might find abundant life in Him. His offer is so counter-intuitive that it just might be crazy enough to be true.

God is pursuing you for this purpose. Not because He needs worshippers (He would get along perfectly well without you) but because He loves you to the point that He would literally lay down His life for your freedom. Love and mercy are actually hunting you down. They will kick down the door if you ask them to because you were not designed to live in prison. Jesus wants more for you than that. The invitation is to cry out for liberation, receive your freedom, and thank your Liberator—no matter how many times you find yourself there. It makes no difference whether you have wasted your entire life moving from one spiritual prison to the next, or if you have tasted freedom only to frequently return to bondage. In either case, we should never be ashamed to approach our Creator and say, "*I need your help! I'm imprisoned. I'm stuck. I'm back here again, for the thousandth time. I didn't mean to end up here, but here I am, can you help me? Can you show me the way to freedom?*" He already knows where you are. He already knows if you are imprisoned. He knows your story and how you ended up there, and Jesus is not ashamed to walk down to the prison and tell the guard . . .

"This one's mine."

***

As flawed human beings, we each tell ourselves our own little story about the universe and what we are doing here, and as a result we have a difficult time grasping God and His goodness (at least I do). Trying to understand the very concept of God can feel unbelievably complex and confusing, but a child can understand the essence of God. Sometimes God is brilliantly simple. For awhile I helped teach Sunday school classes at my church, and I got to interact with a lot of kids who were coming to know God and growing in faith, and I was constantly surprised by how much they were able to grasp.

I remember one particular Sunday that really blew me away. We were getting ready teach a class on God's character, and we wanted the kids to get their minds warmed up before the teaching, so my friend Justin pulled out a white board and a pen and asked them *"who is God?"* Their little hands shot into the air, and before we could even begin to call on them, their answers came flooding in . . . *love!* . . . *Jesus!* . . . *the Creator!* . . . *infinite!* . . . (they were yelling out answers faster than we could write them down) . . . *the Alpha and the Omega!* . . . *the Beginning and the End!* . . . *the Good Shepherd!* . . . *the Father!* . . . (not bad for a couple six-year-olds) . . . *the Lion!* . . . *the Lamb!* . . . *the Truth and the Life!* . . . *our friend!* They must have yelled out fifteen to twenty answers in the first thirty seconds. *"Alright, alright,"* Justin said, *"that's good."* But before he could cut them off completely, one of our little first graders yelled out one final answer that really caught my attention. When asked, *"Who is God?"* this little guy responded with one word:

"Freedom!"

I was stunned. I don't know for sure, but I would like to think that those first graders knew something deep and profound about God. I would like to think their hearts had grasped something beautiful about our spiritual reality. I would like to imagine that at age six they had come to understand a powerful truth about the world we were born into: *the tomb is empty . . . and we never have to be enslaved to anything ever again.*

17 Under the Streetlights

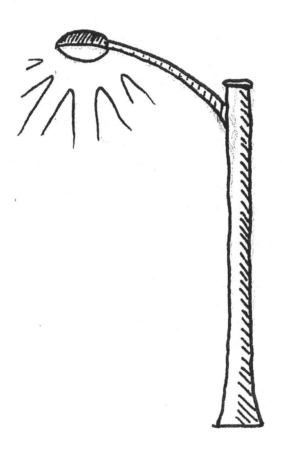

Some people go to their favorite coffee shop when they need to think. Others go to a park, or go for a hike, or go to the gym to work out. Some people play golf, read a book, or have an intimate conversation with friends. Some people just go into their room and shut the door, which works great unless you have roommates. I suppose all those places work well enough, but during my three years of law school when I needed a place to clear my head I would walk to the local cemetery.

Most people think cemeteries are depressing during the day and downright creepy at night, but Riverview Cemetery was different. Well maintained and beautifully designed, Riverview is more like a park than a cemetery. It was built high on a hilltop in southwest Portland, and it overlooks half the city. Well-maintained graves rest under giant oak trees, their rows and columns spreading out in every direction, pouring down the steep hillside and colliding with the surrounding forest. The cemetery itself is huge—the place might be a hundred acres for all I know—and that was part of the joy of it all. A place is always more exciting when there is an element of mystery.

I first discovered the cemetery the night before I started law school. I had just arrived home from my Oregon coast bike trip with Jake, and after unpacking and getting cleaned up, I paced around my neighborhood in nervous anticipation of what the next day would bring. I could not sit still, and I knew I was about to embark on something big. I knew full well that the first year of law school was going to be challenging, and I knew it was going to change me. I knew the professors were going to challenge our way of thinking and attempt rewire our brains to think more like lawyers and less like normal people.

As I mentally prepared for all the changes that lay ahead, I started to wonder what would happen to my newfound faith. I think part of me was worried that in the world of law and logic I would somehow lose my faith altogether. I thought that if my way of thinking and analyzing changed that my perspective on life would begin to change as well, and perhaps my fragile faith would evaporate under the pressures of this new world. I thought that my beliefs were delicate enough to slip through my fingers if I failed to hold on tight. In short, I thought my faith was based on inspiring concepts and I worried that if I stopped being inspired by those ideas my faith would be lost.

As I paced the back streets of my new neighborhood, I stumbled across Riverview Cemetery, hidden away off the beaten path, quiet and undisturbed. I wandered in and sat underneath a giant oak tree, and began to pray honestly about my fears. I prayed that my hope would not be lost. I prayed that I would know God and love Him. I prayed that whatever new and fragile faith I had would not drown in a sea of stress, logic, and skepticism and God responded to my prayers. As I sat underneath that oak tree I felt a deep peace wash over me, the type of peace that can only really come from God's Spirit. As it enveloped me, I knew that God was near and that He was with me in a personal way, and I knew He was going to stick with me through what lay ahead.

Looking back now, I think God was comforting me in that moment. He was reminding me that faith is not fragile, but strong. He was reminding me that faith is about inviting God's Spirit into your heart, and His Spirit is resilient and dynamic. He will never leave us or forsake us, even in our longest trials and darkest nights.

Looking back now I see the beauty of it all. Now I know that when you walk *with* God through trials, you come out with a deeper faith than you ever had before. I think God was whispering to me that night in the cemetery. I think He was reminding me that there was nothing to be afraid of, and that He transcends any obstacle I might face.

After that night I liked the cemetery. I came back often throughout law school, and it quickly became my favorite place to go when I needed to clear my head. Late at night, I would go to the cemetery to pray and watch the streetlights of the city flicker down below. I don't think people are allowed in the cemetery at night, but I figured the dead people wouldn't mind. I am sure they would understand why I had to come. There was a sense of stillness and peace up there, perched above the city and surrounded by forest, and you need moments of peace and stillness in law school. From up there the nearby freeways sounded like distant ocean waves, or the wind gently sweeping through a mountain pass. Everything was quiet. There were no computer screens, or car engines, or static.

Often times I would go up there after a long day of law school, when my head was spinning and sputtering from thinking too much. Leaving my iPhone at home, I would go sit in the silence and look out over the city. From up there, the streetlights looked like ten thousand little embers in the bed of a camp fire; their rows and columns highlighting endless city streets that stretched on for miles in every direction. It was always quiet on my hill. Owls would call longingly to each other, and deer would slowly emerge from the nearby forest, wandering lazily among the graves.

Riverview does not have any streetlights, so for the most part my silent sanctuary was cloaked in darkness, except on rare nights when Portland's clouds would relent; revealing the moon and stars they so diligently conceal. Those were the best nights, sitting under a host of stars with a bed of ten thousand little embers stretched out beneath me, and only the deer and owls to share my secret with.

Every once in a while I would get a cloudless night and the moon would gently flood the cemetery with its soft glow. On moonlit nights, the whole place nearly felt magical. Those were the nights that reminded me why I had come, why I had set aside time to escape the streetlights, emails, and to-do lists, and come to a place where I could see the stars.

Sometimes I forget there are places like that, little hidden places of stillness and solitude. Sometimes I get so wrapped up in the grind of life, rushing from one thing to the next, that I forget there are places of peace. I forget that there is more than the buzz and hum of computer screens, gridlock, and cable TV. I forget that there are places without streetlights. Most of my days are consumed by distractions, and I forget that we were meant to live for more. I forget that there is something weighty, uplifting, and beautiful waiting to be found, if only we take the time to seek it.

I think we were meant to find those places of solitude, and meet with God's Spirit there. I think we were meant to meet with Jesus and be spiritually filled in those places, and we were designed to carry that fullness back into the city—into the streetlights, cubicles, and traffic. We are agents of peace, we are instruments of God's shalom, and we are conduits of God's Light, but most days I act as if my purpose is to answer emails. I needed time on Riverview hill to bring me back.

I had my fair share of beautiful moments there in the stillness of that place, but I remember one night in my sanctuary that was particularly stunning. The constant gray of Portland's fall had given way to a warm starry night, complete with a full moon. It was one of those yellow moons that sits low in the sky and looks unnaturally big, and the cemetery took on new life in its light. I must have sat under my tree for two hours just soaking in the scene (which is a lot of time to devote to anything other than studying or sleep when you are in law school). As I sat and enjoyed in the moment, I prayed over my city. I gazed out over that vast field of streetlights, glowing and twinkling like a bed of dying coals.

Everything looked so distant and peaceful from up on my hill that it would have been easy to forget that life was unfolding down there under those burning embers. It was easy to forget that thousands of people were under those lights, washing their dishes, reading their kids bedtime stories, paying bills, and bickering over the issues of the day. People were answering emails down there and giving goodnight kisses. Maybe even a few of them were praying along with me. I glanced at my watch. It was 10:30pm. Most of them were already sleeping, but plenty of others were lying awake wondering how on earth they were going to make ends meet, or how they were going to get the girl, or any number of the many predicaments that befall our little kingdoms. Life was unfolding down there, under those lights, and I tried to visualize the people going about their lives as I prayed over my city.

There is something really unique about praying in a graveyard, because it brings you face to face with death. It sounds morbid, but I think acknowledging the reality of death is actually a really healthy thing. Visiting my graveyard was always a healthy reminder that life is short, and that this life is ours for just a moment. In the language of Scripture, we are a vapor or a mist, one that is here today and gone tomorrow. In the grand scheme of things we fade really quickly, and acknowledging the brevity of life is healthy (and even exciting) because it gives weight and meaning to each day. Death serves as a stark reminder that every day matters, that our choices matter, and the reality of death is a sobering force which confronts the apathy that plagues us. There is power in acknowledging death because it wakes me up and invites me to re-examine which path I am on and whose glory I am seeking. I think we should be forced to constantly question what we are living for.

The Scriptures say that in the end, only one thing will remain. Everything else that we cling to, worship, and chase after will eventually fade away. In the end the only things that will last, the only things that will withstand the winds of time and echo into eternity are faith, hope, and love—and the greatest of these is love. I should probably tattoo that on my forehead, because most days I do not live as if it were true.

That is why I would go up to my sanctuary, out from under the streetlights, to sit, listen, and remember. I need to be still in order to remember why I am here. I often lose track of that in the city. I lose myself in the noise and traffic, in the flurry of meetings, emails, and final exams. We need time out there in solitude to bring us back. As I walked home that night under a full yellow moon, I left my quiet sanctuary and re-entered the city streets. I came to my first streetlight, a clear sign that I had left the stillness and solitude behind. I stopped to stand under its light, mentally transitioning back to real life, when my attention was drawn to a single moth as it circled and spun wildly under the light. I stopped to watch the drama unfold. The poor moth was desperately out of control, circling up toward the light only to slam into the bulb and spiral wildly back down toward the earth before finally struggling to regain control and begin its next ascent. I watched for a minute or so, standing in the middle of the quiet street. The only sound to be heard was the hum of electricity from the streetlights, and the occasional *whap* of the moth slamming mercilessly into its target. The moth spun in circles, frantic and disoriented. I wanted to invite him out into my sanctuary with me to watch the moon. I wonder if he knew there was a big beautiful moon out there? I wonder if he knew there something real and captivating waiting for him—something more grand and compelling than the streetlight on SW Palatine Hill road?

The Bible sometimes compares people to sheep. I used to think I was really smart, so I did not like being called a sheep. Sheep are dumb and helpless. I used to think the comparison was insulting, but now I think it is beautiful because Jesus is the Good Shepherd, and He cares for His sheep—He blesses them, calls them by name, and guides them in the way they should go. Sheep need to know when danger is coming, because they will literally follow each other off a cliff if they do not have a shepherd. Sheep do really dumb things like that, but I think we can be just as senseless. We need a Shepherd who can see the cliffs coming. We need a God who is willing to come find us when we get lost in the woods—on the days we cannot find our way home and we are being stalked by dark things.

Honestly, it takes a lot of humility for me to admit I am as helpless as a sheep. It takes humility to admit that I am flying blind through life, unable to properly navigate solely on internal wisdom and personal effort. In that sense I really identify with the sheep analogy, but as I walked back into the city on that moonlit night, I realized the truth: I am more like the moth. I actually identified with that miserable little moth circling under the streetlight, because I also get really confused and disoriented, and I end up spending a lot of my time chasing illogical things, not unlike the moth chasing the streetlight on SW Palatine Hill road.

But it runs deeper than that. I have been told that moths are nocturnal and that they normally use the moon as their natural guidance system. The moon serves as a light that they can orient themselves around in order to travel in the darkness. It serves as their own personal north star. Although the moon may fill that function quite well in the untamed wilderness, we all know that modern day moths do not always orient themselves around the moon. More often than not, moths seem to confuse manmade streetlights with the natural light of the moon, and as a result they take up what appears to be a very unhealthy obsession with these lights. I have been told they do this because instinct tells them that the brightest light in the sky must be the moon, and so they attempt to orient their flight around it.[20] As a result we often see moths spinning in circles, seemingly disoriented, risking death in their pursuit of those shiny bulbs.

I think we are remarkably like moths because we do the same thing. We chase lesser things, even worthless things at the risk of our own lives. Something visceral deep down in us tells us to seek. We instinctively seek love, adventure, peace, security, pleasure, glory, and light. The Scriptures tell us that we were made to seek after God and His Light, which was meant to be the calibrating force we orient our lives around. You were designed for this. It was built into your DNA. His Light was meant to be your north star.

If we successfully orient our lives around God—much like the moth that has successfully set his sights on the moon—we have a beautiful, accurate, balanced, and compelling vision of what life is all about and how to navigate it. We are operating on the natural and elemental truth that we were *created* to operate on. This proper orientation gives us incredible clarity as to the meaning of life, and life becomes more fulfilling as a result. We can navigate with accuracy and aptitude. When we tune ourselves to this Light we gain incredible wisdom, insight, and understanding about the nature of our reality, and we have much less to fear. There is a reason that life makes so little sense without God—you were built to know Him. Yet you and I know this is often not how we operate.

Most of us fail to seek after God (or even notice that He exists) and as a result we orient our lives around

---

[20] If this isn't true, please do not tell me, for it would surely kill an already strained analogy.

something less than God's grace and glory. This is not unlike the moth that mistakenly orients himself around a lesser light. You see, streetlights in the world of moths are remarkably like sin and idolatry in the world of men. To see how this is so, we have to consider what a streetlight must look like to a moth. In their eyes the streetlights must look big, bright, and enticing. They are tangible, near, and exciting. Their buzz and hum is comforting and accessible. Their light calls and beckons, and they are available for enjoyment three hundred and sixty five days a year. They are completely reliable, predictable, and plentiful. They are created, artificial, and foreign to the original habitat of the moth, but they have enormous draw and power. When you are directly under them, the moon is eclipsed and forgotten; it is distant and dim by comparison. While the streetlights will always come on, the moon reveals itself on its own time. Maybe the moon will come out tonight—maybe not. Maybe it will reveal its full self—maybe not. The moon's gravity and presence are always constant, but its visibility is anything but. Will the moon reveal itself tonight? The moths just have to wait and see.

We can say similar things about you and God.

Sin and idolatry are somewhat "unnatural" occurrences in God's creation. They are something introduced from outside of God's heart and intent. The Scriptures start with humanity in a perfect garden, and point forward to our future in a perfect garden-like city, neither of which have room for sin, idolatry, or death. These things are outside of God's heart, and they do not exist in an ideal human world where God rules and reigns.

From our perspective, sin is close, big, bright, and certainly enticing; so much of sin's temptation stems from the fact that it is tangible and near. We can have it right now, anytime we want, three hundred and sixty five days a year. In a culture built on instant gratification, the allure is almost too much to resist. The pleasure of sin feels reliable, predictable, and safe.

Sin is real and powerful and close, and when it consumes us it blots out and eclipses God. It can so thoroughly consume our perspective and flood our vision, that sadly God is eclipsed and feels distant, removed, and dim by comparison. When we indulge in our sin and bury ourselves in it, we often fail to hear God's voice. This eclipsing sensation is not unlike the blinding of a moth that has been consumed by its favorite streetlight and forgotten about the moon. The moon has not moved an inch. It has not hidden itself or withdrawn and is as near as ever, but the moth has blinded itself to the moon and forgotten about it completely.

To make matters worse, the lesser lights that we love to orient our lives around are accessible and predictable, and we turn to them for regular and consistent comfort and security. God on the other hand, will reveal himself on His time, not ours. God's presence and gravity are unchanging, but His visibility (i.e. our *experience* of God) is anything but. Perhaps He will reveal himself tonight, perhaps not. We just have to wait and see. I have been following Jesus for nearly a decade, and the movements of His Spirit are about as predictable to me as the weather in Portland. I do not have a clue what the weather is going to be like tomorrow. I have no idea if I will be able to see the stars or not. I have no idea if the moon will light up my hilltop sanctuary. Chances are it will rain. But the streetlights on the other hand? I can guarantee you they will be on, and I can even tell you where to find them and what time they will come on and how long they will stay on.

Whether we like it or not, each and every night the world predictably flips on the streetlights. They are too numerous to count. They line the freeways and overwhelm the stars. They shine powerfully, each demanding our heart's attention. The streetlights come in many forms, but they include corrupted sexuality, greed, fear, pride, self-centeredness, and lust. There is a streetlight for every destructive habit and every form of substance abuse. We make streetlights out of conceit, bitterness, anxiety, religion, judgmentalism, power, respect, and possessions. We make streetlights out of family, reputation, food, and security. We turn them into little gods that rule our lives and hold the deepest place in our hearts.

Our streetlights are the thing we choose to idolize and orient our lives around. They are often everyday things that we turn into ultimate things. They are the thing to which we devote most of our free time and attention. Not all of them are inherently bad, in fact, many of them are good things that God created, but there is an allure and temptation in our hearts that begs us to make them ultimate things. We are tempted to take good things and make them "god things." We fashion them into little idols by turning them into our own personal streetlights that rule over our lives. They inform and color every action and decision we make—guiding and shaping our thoughts. They are the comforts we run back to again and again. They are the distractions we love so much, and the natural desire of our hearts is to cling to them and worship lesser things.

Like the lights of Vegas, our streetlights call to us promising fulfillment and leaving us broken. They pull on our hearts like gravity, beckoning us with desire and passion and luring us with a thousand tempting promises. They scream at us through a cacophony of lies and static; through a myriad of voices, advertisements, and white noise. They have catchy taglines and they call to us with deadly persuasiveness. They come in a thousand styles and sizes, but they have the same effect: they all tend to blot out the moon. Each of them competes for your allegiance and the best of your time and attention. Each of them wants to be worshipped.

We all feel the tug of their call, but if you draw near to them, center your life around them, and stand directly under their light, several things will happen. The first is that God (*the* Light) will be eclipsed by sin and streetlights. Sin will feel close, bright, and illusively powerful in comparison. The idols are in your face. The second thing that happens is that you end up staring up into the spiritual equivalent of a bright fluorescent bulb, which typically leaves you with a pounding headache and very little inspiration.

The alternative to all this is that we orient our lives around Jesus, who (to extend the analogy) is the great moon of humanity. You see, you and I were born into a dark world ruled by sin. In fact, this fallen world is (spiritually speaking) an endless night in which we have never seen the sun, just as no one has ever seen the Father. There is only One who knows the Father and perfectly reveals His character to the world. Jesus was sent from the Father and He became fully human, limited Himself and yet still acting as a perfect *reflection* of the Father. He was a dim reflection of the Light that is God.

In the same way, anyone born into an endless dark night, though never having seen the sun directly would occasionally see a reflection of its light from the moon. Jesus is nothing less than the Light of the world shining in the darkness. He is a bright and vibrant moon that sheds its soft light in an otherwise darkened night. He is a dim reflection of the Father, though only dim in terms of *quantity*, not quality. The reflection is perfect in its accuracy, but limited in its magnitude.

Moonlight is the same way. It is the exact same *type* of light as sunlight; it is of the same nature and it is from the same source. Moonlight is still sunlight, only filtered and reflected through a different medium. In the same way, Jesus is a direct reflection of God's character and heart. He is a direct reflection of the Light, only filtered through a different medium. Jesus is God filtered through the lens of *human*. He is infinite and eternal Spirit expressed through a physical person.

In our spiritual landscape of streetlights we have underestimated the beauty of the moon, and misjudged just how beautiful Jesus is. We have underestimated the influence, presence, beauty, and gravitational pull of God in the here and now. Somewhere along the way we lost the plotline, and we lost track of God's beauty. Jesus came to reclaim it. Jesus came from the Father to point us back to the glory and beauty of God, simultaneously exposing the futility of our streetlights. He made it really clear that there are corrupted distractions that have been dazzling us since the dawn of humanity. Greed, power, and depraved sexuality leave us spinning, disoriented, and empty, and Jesus knew we would be tempted to waste our lives chasing them.

Jesus knew we would want to chase and worship our streetlights for the same reason that moths do: the streetlights mimic the moon. In other words, our streetlights mimic the true God of our hearts. Each of us has our own weaknesses, idols, and temptations, but there is more at play here than just temptations and compromise. I think we are clinging to twisted substitutes for God Himself. We gravitate toward our streetlights because we see in them the very qualities of God. We find hints of God's goodness in our knock-offs and substitutes, and that is why we fall so hard for them and pursue them so stubbornly. Our broken and deceptive parodies contain small glimmers of the glory, excitement, peace, security, and love we were meant to find in our Creator, and even small glimmers can capture our hearts.

In fact, our temptations, idols, and streetlights are the things we turn to for salvation, only we do not call it salvation. We hold on to this desperate hope that they will bring us the contentment and joy we so desperately desire. We turn to our streetlights for comfort, hope, security, and identity. We look to them for shalom, wholeness, love, and empowerment. We are quick to turn to lesser things and demand that they give us what only God can really give. We will worship our spouses, our children, our successes, or even fancy cars—anything that will give us the slightest taste of the good things God has for us. We rarely call it worship, but that is exactly what it is.

We look to the streetlights to complete us, to make us feel more alive, to make us feel powerful, to give us worth, and to fill a deep void in us. We long for them to scratch our deep-seated itch. We will turn to anything but God to give us a taste of what God offers. We will elevate anything to His position for even the pettiest of payouts. Functionally, we live as if we can make better gods than God.

Moths do the same thing. They orient their existence around streetlights precisely because streetlights have some of the same *qualities* as the moon. They are seeking after light all along; they just get fooled by the rip offs. They are chasing the wrong light. The streetlights are supplying phony imitations of the real thing. They are parodies and caricatures of something authentic and satisfying. Our streetlights are so overwhelmingly tempting because they can predictably give us a shadowy sample of the good things we were designed to find in our Creator. If moths can teach us anything, it is that orienting ourselves around the knock-offs lands us in a desperate place. You and I (like the moths) will be disoriented, blinded, and misled. We will operate on faulty and self-serving assumptions, and even be willing deceive ourselves in pursuit of our predictable parodies. In our profound desperation we compromise our deepest integrity, and yet in the end we are not satisfied. What you are looking for is *the* Light and it will not help you or anyone else if you settle for an imitation.

We were meant to orient ourselves around something greater, and to calibrate our lives off something divine. When we operate on that frequency by acting in step with God's Spirit and living in the light of His future Kingdom, we will act in a way that does not make sense to the world and its standard operating procedures.

In the years following Jesus' death and resurrection, countless people were put to death for following Him. To the atheist this would seem a cruel and twisted fate: to be cheated out of your very life because you were delusional enough to believe this man. After all, this life is all we have! What a shame to throw it all away on some Rabbi and his lies. It conjures up modern day horror stories about cults and mass suicide. Dying for something that you can't see? Well that is just downright dangerous. The notion of it makes most people uneasy. It makes others downright angry. It makes me smile a little. These people had seen something. They carried a hope stronger than death. How many people do you know who would pin their entire lives on a "maybe," a hoax, or a fraud? Most of those who stood face to face with the resurrected Jesus wanted to see Him again on the other side of their own deaths, and they oriented their lives around that hope.

They oriented their lives around something the world does not grasp or understand, and it caused them to operate in a manner the world finds completely illogical. They acted in tandem with something higher—something heavenly. This was confusing to everyone living on the street level who centered their lives around the streetlights. To everyone stumbling around under the lesser lights living in darkness and believing life was all about them, the life and death of these Jesus followers did not compute. The facts simply did not add up. A light shone in the darkness, but the darkness did not understand it.

In the eyes of the world life is about self-promotion, and because this life is all you have you must *always* act in the name of self-preservation, even at the great expense of others. This is the script the world hands us.

This was the backdrop for a very curious scene in which people were giving up their lives for their faith. It was into this self-centered world that countless people denied themselves and gave up the right to build their own little kingdoms for the benefit of His. It is over and against this modern mindset that countless millions have stood firm in their faith.

Those first followers (and countless millions since) decided they would rather be put to death than give up Jesus. In the eyes of the world this seems completely backwards, but so does everything else that Jesus did and said. He says it is through His bondage that we are set free; He said it is through His brokenness that we are made whole; He claims it is through His wounds that we find healing. He claims that if we die to ourselves we will find true life. He claims that the greatest among us should be a servant to all, and that those who have most will be become the least, and the least of this age will become the greatest. He claims that those who want to keep and promote their lives over everything else will ironically be the ones to lose their lives, but the one is willing to die to their selfish desires for His sake will find it. It all sounds upside down and backwards because He was preaching about the glory of the moon in a world of streetlights. He seemed confusing and different because He was operating on a different frequency. He had oriented His life around an alternative source of light. He was calibrating His guidance system around a different star, and He invites us to do the same.

Unfortunately we are confused, overwhelmed, and human, so we pursue the streetlights. If we pursue them with reckless disregard, without restraint or reservation, and allow them to consume us, we will meet the same fate as the overzealous moth who flings himself headlong into the nearest fluorescent bulb. We receive death (physical and spiritual) as our final reward. A moth will circle the light and draw closer and closer until it is consumed by its object, and we should be careful not to follow the same pattern with our greatest streetlights and temptations.

Have you ever just sat and watched a moth chase a light bulb? The whole scene is ridiculous. I am almost annoyed as I watch it circle the light, moving toward its own death with such reckless determination. I can almost imagine what the creature must be thinking . . . *"If I can just a little closer . . . c'mon . . . just a little closer and everything will be better... I've almost got it!"* From an outsider's perspective their behavior is completely foolish, and it is by definition suicidal.

But before we curse the moths for being so shortsighted, we have to recognize that we often do the same thing. *"C'mon,"* we think, *"if I can just get a little wealthier . . . everything would be better . . . I just need a little more money."* Doesn't sound like you? There are plenty of other streetlights. *"If I can just get a little prettier . . . a little stronger . . . a little more powerful . . . a little more popular . . . maybe if I could just get a little more religious . . . then everything would be great."* We think that if we could just marry *that* person, buy *that* house, or get *that* promotion everything will be better. We are chasing streetlights.

I will admit that it is difficult for me to worship the unseen over the seen. It is difficult for us to give up our streetlights in order to take hold of the life God offers us, but on the other hand, we simply cannot allow ourselves to be content with half-hearted living. God does not want a bunch of children who settle for "good enough" or "just scraping by" or "I'm surviving." He wants us to have the best life, and I am not talking about the American dream. I am talking about a genuine life filled with a type of joy that MTV knows nothing about. God wants us to delight in Him, and partner with Him to do great things in the world. This is the grand and sweeping vision that spans from the genesis of humanity through the eternal Age to Come.

There is a dangerous side effect to orienting our lives around lesser lights: we assume our purpose is artificially small. We assume our lives are insignificant, boring, and very limited in scope. Our lives boil down to a few short years that we get to spend on Earth with our idol, and nothing else really matters. We assume our lives have no lasting impact or meaning beyond the few short years that we get to fill with pleasure or pain, and we begin to operate on those assumptions. Of course we are living a lie, and life tends to become self-destructive as a result, but once again we have the moths to keep us company.

The disoriented moth probably assumes that the only meaningful space in the world is the eighteen feet between the ground and the streetlight it is currently chasing. That becomes the total scope of its life, and nothing else matters. Everything else is out of sight and out of mind. They are blind to the grandeur of the world and the depth and beauty of the reality they live in. In that moment they have forgotten all the magnificence that exists outside their little bubble. They forget what an incredible world is unfolding around them. The moth has become consumed with the idol of its heart. It has been captivated by sin and become shortsighted and confused as a result.

We do this all the time when we settle for the streetlights of our world, because we fool ourselves into believing in an artificially cramped version of reality. The streetlight story is a simple one, which is far less fulfilling than the creation-wide story God invites us to embrace. To make matters worse, the streetlights do not hold a candle to an authentic relationship with God built on faith. God is much more richly complex and more deeply fulfilling than anything we would replace Him with. After all, how could you really compare the beauty of the moon with a row of streetlights?

The moon is massive, vibrant, captivating, and even romantic. It effortlessly pushes aside the dark night with its soft and radiant glow, graces a thousand desert valleys and mountaintop meadows, and brings a sense of peace and tranquility. The moon has a gentle majesty to it—a steadfast and unwavering faithfulness. It stabilizes our orbit and tugs gently on our oceans. The moon has a mysterious and untamed beauty to it. That radiant orb hangs suspended in our sky, a thousand miles beyond our reach, beckoning to us. It captured our hearts in such a way that we moved heaven and earth (risking our lives and billions of dollars) just to walk on it. The moon is part of our frontier and our folklore; it is as beautiful as it is mysterious.

God was meant to hold the same place in our hearts. He was meant to capture our imaginations in such a way that we would move heaven and earth (or at least come out from under the streetlights) just to gaze upon Him, to admire Him and draw near to Him. God gently tugs on our reality by stabilizing all of the life in the universe and wooing us with a steadfast and faithful love. His radiant glow graces billions of hearts, and He longs to grace billions more. All the streetlights on Earth would not be worth a portion of the majesty of the moon, nor would all of our idols and life-sized distractions be worth even a fraction of the glory of God. The two are incomparable. The world offers us cheap alternatives, knock-offs, and rip-offs that leave us starving for something that will truly satisfy. We want something that will bring us to life and send electricity buzzing through our veins. We want to feel empowered and safe. We want to feel dangerous and bold. We want to feel accomplished and loved. We want to feel valued and valuable. We want to feel sought after and wanted. We want to be known and accepted, but because we are human (and confused) we look in all the wrong places. We wander from place to place, and it usually isn't long before we end up staring into the face of a streetlight, dazzled and awestruck, and begin living a lie.

What God desires is real and authentic relationship. He wants you to be part of His family. He wants to speak blessing and truth over you. He wants you to be part of His eternity. He wants to be known by you in the here and now, and those things cannot happen when we are stuck under the streetlights, steeped in confusion and consumed by the object of our lust. It cannot happen when we chase empty alternatives in vain.

Too often we cling to our idols. We cling to lesser things, sometimes even good things, at the expense of experiencing the *best* things. Good things are good, but they are no replacement for God, and our Creator is not the God of good, He is the God of *best*. He does not approach us to offer things that are simply good or "good enough." He is not out to sell us a slightly better product. Jesus does not offer us a mediocre alternative to otherwise equally good ways of living our lives; He offers us the best life. He offers us the best things. He offers us nothing short of Himself. He offers us a way of living that can only be described as "life that is truly life" because there are no other words describe it. God has been relentlessly loving and pursuing this broken world because He cannot stand to see us continually dominated, ripped off, and enslaved by streetlights.

I imagine when God searched the earth He saw a lot of people—His image bearers, the vessels designed to hold and reflect His love—staring up into the streetlights, blinded and confused. He saw a whole lot of streetlight addicts and too few saints. He saw too much strife and not enough peace. He saw too much slavery and not enough joy. He saw too many streetlights and not enough stargazers, and *our God is not ok with that*. His love and compassion are far too dynamic and active to sit on the sidelines.

God did not create us for the streetlights, and He knew full well they were not going to disappear anytime soon. He could have reacted in any number of righteously angry or even violent ways, but instead His response was to send His son for us. Jesus stepped into humanity, came down to the street level, and got to work telling a bunch of very confused "moths" about the glory of the "moon" and all the ways we were intended to live. Jesus saw the streetlights just as we do, but He was not fooled by them. Instead, He invited us to flood our eyes with His Light, leaving the cheap alternatives behind. He explained that many of us are filling our eyes with unhealthy light, which ends up being more like darkness than light. He said that when we fill our eyes with the knock-off lights, our whole bodies end up being filled with darkness, and when we fill our eyes with false fluorescent light and we think it is authentic light, we are in the worst darkness of all. Meaning that if we fill our eyes with streetlights, and we think we have God's Light, we have become terribly lost. If we believe that the false lights of modern moralism, intellectualism, the new atheism, or the nearest streetlight are actually *the* Light, we are in the worst shape of all.

Jesus revealed the depth of our lostness, exposed the severity of the human condition, and then issued an invitation: *follow me.* Follow me out from under the streetlights and out of your city of sin. Follow me off the streets, and up into the hills. Follow me out from under the fluorescent knock-offs and into the mountains that surround your city of white noise and static. He invites us to find some high sanctuary. From up there we begin to see how small and powerless the city lights are below. As our eyes begin to adjust to our newfound freedom, we begin to notice the beauty of the moon. We finally begin to gaze on God and grasp His true size and glory.

After we come out from under the streetlights it takes our eyes some time to readjust. It takes time for the blinding headache to wear off and the sensitivity to return to our eyes and our hearts. It takes time to reorient ourselves around the moon. The transition requires great patience, and we are often tempted to run back to what is tangible. We may continue to feel the tug and lure of the streetlights, and our temptations may still call to us with accessibility and allure, but the longer we stay on the mountain the more we fall in love with the moon.

If we never spend time on the mountain, and we never respond to Jesus' invitation to leave the streetlights behind, it is all too easy to get lost in our sins and distractions and forget why we are here. Only in His freedom do we find the space to soberly acknowledge that we have the sovereign choice to devote our lives to God or the streetlights. Only from a high sanctuary do we find the wisdom to recognize that one of the two will ultimately fade to the sands of time. The streetlights will burn out and fall into disrepair long before the moon stops sharing its light. The question then becomes, which one will we live for? Because the sobering truth is that *we will share the fate of the one we follow.* There is a reason that the invitation of Jesus is always "follow me" instead of "believe in me": because orientation matters. He does not want to be a footnote in your life, or the right answer on a spiritual test, but He wants to be the Light that you center your life around. That is the difference between believing and following: it is a matter of orientation.

I think the average streetlight-loving moth believes in the moon, but it is merely a technical belief. The moth would not (when soberly confronted) deny that the moon exists—that fact is lodged somewhere in its little moth brain—but this technical belief does not change that fact that it is essentially consumed by the streetlights. In the same way, it is quite easy to believe in God in some dry technical sense, all the while orienting our lives around something else completely. We can believe in God while worshipping something that will fade away. This is the difference between believing and following, and the Scriptures make it clear that they are not the same. Even the demons believe in God, and tremble. Apparently demon theology is spot on, but they orient themselves around the darkest of lights, and they will be destroyed along with the streetlights at the end of the age.

We are confronted with this choice of who and what to follow. Tomorrow you will wake up face to face with the streetlights, with their predictable light luring you and their electric hum gently calling to you, but if you accept God's invitation to rise above them and avoid those blinding headaches, you will catch a glimpse of what matters most.

Consider the alternative: you can stand like a deer in the headlights (or the streetlights, or the cathode rays) and miss your invitation. You might miss the invitation to leave the mundane and ordinary behind and to be filled by God's Spirit and live by His strength. When we orient our lives around the God of the Universe, something fascinating happens. God's Spirit fills our hearts, and the streetlights begin to lose their power over us. Their overwhelming appeal begins to fade, and our very desire to be consumed by them is lost. Their power to tempt us begins to wither, and we become increasingly empowered to live under the streetlights without *belonging* to them. We begin to live in a new and liberated fashion—being in the world but not *of* it. This is the invitation we've been offered, and if the thought of missing the invitation means nothing to us, it is probably because we misunderstand the gravity of what we are being invited into.

We are being invited into a whole new type of life. You are invited to pull up the anchor and set your sights on the skyline *because His Kingdom is coming.* It is out there, over the horizon, out of sight beyond the curve of the earth and the space and time that still separate us. The moon has shown us much in this otherwise dark and endless night, but we must never forget that we are still waiting for the dawn.

18 The Dawn

MATT DEISEN

**"Arise, shine, for your light has come, and
the glory of the Lord rises upon you.
See, darkness covers the earth and thick
darkness is over the peoples, but the Lord
rises upon you and his glory appears over
you. Nations will come to your light, and
kings to the brightness of your dawn."**

– Isaiah 60v1-3

I f we were born into an endless night, with the moon
and streetlights competing for our attention, then the
good news of the Scriptures is that there is going to
be a dawn. A New Age is going to begin, and we believe
it because Jesus was a signpost pointing forward to it.
His life was a foretaste of the coming Kingdom. What
happened in and through Jesus is going to happen again,
only bigger. His resurrection was the spark that lit a new
fire and opened up a whole new world of possibilities,
because if Jesus actually rose from the dead as a historic
event in time-space history, then you can too. A new
order is coming, and Jesus said that His followers can
expect to be resurrected into it. Jesus is the first fruit—a
foreshadowing of this future event. He is a blueprint and
a pattern of what is to come. This is the uncontainable
hope we celebrate. This is the contagious message Jesus
came to deliver. This is why Jesus gracing humanity was
the the most important event in time-space history.

He launched an invasion of the Kingdom of Light in
the middle of our current corrupted age, and now we get
glimpses of heaven on Earth. These glimpses not only act
as gifts in the night, but they also serve as a reminder that

in the grand scheme of our universe *there will be a dawn*. Right now we only know the night, but into the darkness a light shone. That light was the light for all humanity, and that light had flesh and blood—He had a name and dwelt among us—and now we know there will be a dawn. The dawn will be glorious, and you and I have no idea just how glorious it will be because we have never tasted direct sunlight. But we know the sun exists.

How do we know the sun exists as we sit in darkness? It illuminates the moon! The moon sheds its light, night after night, and the only explanation is that the sun is out there, somewhere beyond the curve of the earth and the space and time that still separate us. How do we know the Father exists? He illuminates the Son and raised Him from the dead! What God did in and through Jesus is meant to show the world that He exists. That is half the point. We look forward to the dawn with hope and expectation because we have seen the moon and the moonlight demands an explanation.

I mentioned before that Jesus is a perfect reflection of the Father, only dimmer. He was the same nature and *quality* as the Father, only in a smaller *quantity*. This is a necessary result of what happens when an infinite God becomes human, when the universal becomes particular, and when something incomprehensible expresses Himself in a way we can easily grasp. Jesus is a dim reflection of the Father, just as moonlight is a dim reflection of the sun and the day to come. The moon produces no light of its own, but only reflects the sunlight from another source. In the same way, Jesus did and spoke nothing on His own steam, but rather He only did and said what the Father was doing and saying. He was an obedient reflection.

The moon reflects the same *type* of light as the sun, only limited in its quantity. As a result, it serves as a signpost pointing forward to the real source of light that will come at dawn. Jesus, among other things, was a signpost pointing forward to the sunrise, a preview of the Age to Come, and a small sampling of God's Kingdom. When it comes in full, as the great Dawn of the New Heavens and New Earth, we should expect a whole new magnitude of Light and energy that we can hardly imagine.

Just as sunlight defines the day, the Age to Come will be defined and marked by Jesus' rule and reign. God will *be* our Light. The Light that is coming is similar in quality to the light we have already witnessed, but the nature and magnitude of what is coming is more than we can comprehend. Remember the God who is full of light, surrounded by angels who sing of His uncontainable majesty? We are going to see that God face to face. All the miracles and raising people from the dead, all the relentless love and unconditional forgiveness, that is all a small glimpse of the type of life and power that we will experience in His Kingdom. We get a dim taste of it now. The healing we see coming through Jesus and His followers is a small sampling of the abundant and holistic healing that we will experience in that future place. They serve as glimmers on the horizon—so faint and small that if you lived your secular life and never stopped to look up, you would miss them completely. But those who know what's come search the distant skies and we see a light creeping in; almost too dim to perceive, but undeniably present.

For now we live in the darkness and wrestle with the streetlights. The moon is here with us, giving us a taste of what is to come, and the moon is far greater than our streetlights will ever be. It is present and accessible, but never overbearing, while extending a gentle invitation for anyone with the passion and patience to seek it. Yet even the moon of this age is sporadic and difficult to predict. While it is faithful and dependable in its existence and nearness, it is also soft and irregular in its light. As a result, the streetlights rule most of humanity. The fluorescent kingdom of darkness has enormous hold and sway over our world, but it will not always be so.

One day God is going to shut down the grid. One day God is going to go straight to the source of the streetlights and pull the plug. He is going to cut the mainline to the whole system, purging the world of evil in the process. These events may very well be shocking and violent, but for those who oriented their lives around the "moon" it will be both welcomed and necessary, because God promises that after the streetlights are shut down there will be a sunrise—a great and glorious dawn—a Light so bright and so beautiful that even if the streetlights were still functioning they would be small and dim by comparison. Their dim fluorescent glow would be unnoticeable in a world flooded with living and divine Light, and they would be so insignificant in the new sunlight that you would never want to go back to them again. Even if the streetlights were left on, they would lose their grip entirely, offering only an obnoxious buzz and insignificant light. They would mean nothing in the brilliant sunshine of the world to come, when the whole earth is flooded with the knowledge of the glory of God.

Imagine the first sunrise in a land that had only known darkness. Imagine that your eyes had adjusted to moonlight and streetlights, and then the first sunrise came crashing into your dark world. If you had never seen a sunrise before, you would probably think the whole world was ending. You would think that our entire planet was being lit on fire. It would be terrifying and yet incomprehensibly beautiful. You would tremble with fear and uncertainty and your skin would tingle with awe. That first sunrise would no doubt be true and clear. It would be cloudless and breathtaking. You would be shaken to the core of your being, for it would appear to be the end of all things, and yet you would sense somewhere deep down in your heart that it was also the beginning. Perhaps you would sense without words that all things were about to be made new.

This is the dawn we anticipate. In the meantime, we are invited to live with that hope, but too few of us do. Our collective skepticism holds us back. We think to ourselves, *"How terribly naïve to believe in something like a renewed world. After potentially billions of years of our material universe existing as it has, you really expect me to believe that some God we can't see or touch or prove is going to magically step in and change everything?"*

Yes.

I believe that. I hope in that, and you can too. Here's why: the fact that you exist is statistically almost impossible. According to scientific estimates there is only a one in many trillion chance that you should be alive at all. Our universe should not be able to support anything bigger than bacteria. In a universe governed by random chance and chaos, you should not be here in the first place. None of this should be here, but it is. Which means we are already standing knee deep in evidence of a creative power that we can't grasp or understand. And if the universe were created on purpose, you would have every reason to hope.

A self-created universe could spontaneously change, but if we accept that God created it and is still in the picture (which is the only way to explain Jesus' life, death, and resurrection) then the chances of God following through on His promise is a lot greater than one in several trillions. It would be a near certainty. A self-created universe could (theoretically) spontaneously change in nature, but once we accept the existence of a Creator, it becomes infinitely plausible. In fact, recreating the universe would actually take *less* creative genius and cosmic engineering than original creation. Meaning that the launch of the New Heavens and New Earth will almost be easier than original birth. In that sense, the idea of God coming to remake and renew the world is actually more plausible than it first appears. It is (statistically speaking) more likely than Genesis. The "impossible" act was you and I—it is *this* reality. Breathing new life into old bones is easier to grasp than inventing bones in the first place. Changing the rules that govern everything seems easier than creating the rules and the stuff in the first place. Perhaps we should trust God to do it. In my atheism it sounded impossible, but if God can paint such a beautiful picture as this one, do you think we could trust Him to restore it? If God built this car from scratch in His garage, do you think we could trust Him to renovate it? If Jesus built this house with His bare hands, do you think we could trust Him to remodel it as well? I think we can. The first performance gives ample evidence to suggest that an encore can occur.

But in all of this I am speaking only of probability, creative energy, and God's capacity. I am simply arguing that God *can* do it and that He is capable of it. Believing that God *will* actually do it is a totally different story. That requires a different type of trust, one that is born out of intimate relationship. The more we know Jesus on a personal level, the more we will trust in His promises, and I think we need both in order to overcome our skepticism; we need to grasp God's capacity in our heads *and* we need to trust Jesus' promises in our hearts. Without both, the concept of recreation feels impossibly out of reach.

The irony is that we sit in a reality that is statistically nearly impossible and point our fingers toward the future with skepticism saying *"That can't happen! That's impossible!"* Yet even as we think these thoughts we are sitting in the more unlikely of the two realities. Statistically speaking, there was less of a chance of this world occurring than the next. If anything should take the brunt of our skepticism, perhaps it should be the world right in front of us.

The only reason we do not question our current reality is because it is already here, and the only reason we can so passionately deny that Jesus will return to usher in a new reality is because we haven't seen it yet. Recreation has not happened yet, and therefore we feel justified in proclaiming that it never will. This is one of the pitfalls of the scientific worldview. Our reality has obeyed a set of laws and behaved a certain way for as long as we have been around to observe it (or at least as long as we have been keeping track) and therefore we conclude that the universe has always acted this way, and always will.

But the whole reason we are excited about God's promise and the gospel of Jesus is that He is announcing something new that has never happened before. The whole point is that recreation is unexpected, and it is so radically different from the rest of the human history that we could never have predicted it ourselves. That's why it's good *news*. Of course science cannot predict or understand it, because it hasn't been witnessed yet! But rest assured the dawn is coming, and God clued us in because He wants us to have hope. We were built to anticipate it. In fact, the Scriptures say that all of creation is yearning for the day when God's glory is finally revealed, and you and I were built to yearn along with it.

In the meantime, we live in hopeful anticipation of that future. We are invited to break the chains that bind us. Jesus gives us permission to cut the anchors that weigh us down and let out the sails. We are invited to come up out of the city, leaving our streetlights and rip-offs behind. We are invited to embrace the adventure and live for God's in-breaking Kingdom right here and now. We are invited to open our hearts and minds to the incredible reality that would exist if Jesus were telling the truth. God is poised on the edge of His seat, eager to blow us away. All we need is the faith to let down the sails.

19 Going All In

Risk is an essential element of adventure, making courage a prerequisite of exploration. We cannot explore new lands unless we are willing to leave familiar shores in pursuit of the horizon.

I have always questioned the legitimacy of poker as a sport. I played on a lot of different sports teams growing up, and none of them required you to sit as still as possible. My friend John watches poker on ESPN, which makes poker seem like a real sport, but I am convinced it's not. From what I can tell the goal is to wear a baseball cap and move as little as possible. There is almost no visible action at all, and yet thousands of people tune in to watch the drama unfold. The tension around the poker table is palpable, and people like my friend John are drawn in by it. From what I gather, most of the tension is derived from the fact that millions of dollars are at stake, and if a player twitches their eyebrow at the wrong time they might lose.

Who doesn't love a high stakes game loaded with mystery and full of surprise endings? I can understand the intrigue. We love watching people play the odds, betting their life savings and waiting for the right moment to strike. That's the sport of it I guess: managing odds, taking risks, and betting big at the right moment. To be honest, I am a little jealous of professional poker players, because part of me wishes I could sit around a table, nod a couple of times, and walk away with a million dollars. I am convinced people watch poker for that reason. Not all of us can slam-dunk on a ten-foot hoop, but everyone knows how to sit at a table with a baseball cap on, and who doesn't secretly wish they had a million dollars?

I have always wondered what I would do with that kind of money. I doubt I will ever be rich, but it is fun to think about. I wonder if the money would rule over me and corrupt me, or if I would actually be able to rule over the money and do beautiful things with it. I wonder if I would use it to help bring justice to the earth. I wonder if I could take the road less traveled—walking in God's holiness, embodying God's uniqueness—and have a million dollars at the same time. It is a valid question because most people in America are probably a lot like me (in that they would love to have a million dollars), but if you cannot own a million dollars and walk in what God has for you at the same time, then wishing for a million dollars is a huge waste of time.

There is a really well known passage of Scripture where a rich young man approaches Jesus. He asks Jesus the million-dollar question, the one seated at the center of our thoughts on God and spirituality. He asks Jesus, "What must I do to inherit eternal life?"[21] The two of them talk about following the commandments and putting God first, and it turns out the rich young guy does all the right stuff. He is a morally responsible person and perhaps even a religious all-star.

But then the young man proceeds to ask Jesus another question. He asks Jesus if he still lacks anything. He asks Jesus if there is something else out there for him to engage in or some other adventure in life that he has yet to embark on. At least I think that is what he was asking, because Jesus tells him that if he really wants to live a full life—if he really wants to be perfect—he should sell what

---

[21] Luke 18:18.

he has, use the money to bring justice to the earth, and then come and follow Him. Jesus invites the young man to loosen his grip on earthly possessions, cut the anchors that are tying him down, and to set out for new horizons. Jesus invites him to lighten his burden, drop the sails, and engage in the adventure that He offers.

But instead the rich man very famously walks away, and he is pretty bummed out as he goes, because he knows he doesn't have the guts to give up what he has. He lacks the gusto to make the exchange and trade earthly things for heavenly things. I think deep in his own heart the rich man knows he is missing out, but he cannot bring himself to accept the invitation, and has no choice but to walk away. I think the rich young man was sad because he sensed deep down that his wealth owned him, and he knew it was keeping him from something better.

After the young man leaves, Jesus talks to the crowd that has gathered, and He teaches them that it is actually really hard for the rich to enter the Kingdom of Heaven. He compares it to a camel passing through the eye of a needle. Most of us like to skip this passage because we live in America, and by the world's standards most of us are rich. It makes us uncomfortable to think we might have to choose between wealth and God. It makes you wonder what Jesus was getting at.

At first glance, Jesus seems to be announcing that only people of a certain tax bracket are eligible to participate in God's Kingdom, but I don't think that's the case. It is true that the poor often have to rely on God for daily bread, and poverty brings those with open hearts closer to the Father by strengthening their faith. It is also true that those of us who are wealthy and comfortable seem less likely to humble ourselves before God, but I think Jesus is getting at something deeper.

The easiest way for me to understand what Jesus was teaching the rich young man is to picture my life as a poker game. I only played poker a handful of times growing up, and I was never particularly good at it, but the interesting thing about my poker game was that the more chips I had, the harder it was to take big risks. The higher my pile, the less likely I was to go all in. The more I collected, the more cautious I became.

In the same way, the more we accumulate in this life, the more we have to lose. Generally speaking, the more money we have, the less risky we become, and our money can become a direct obstacle to living the life Jesus calls us to. To make matters worse, some of us make tremendous sacrifices in order to gain more wealth. We are willing to sacrifice our relationships, our integrity, and even our relationship with God in order to achieve our material ends. But the more we sacrifice to attain our wealth, the more weight and value we assign to it. The more costly it was to get something, the greater the value it holds in our eyes, and if our wealth ever grows so significant as to become a part of our identity, it becomes all the harder to give away. All the sudden reckless living is out of the question. Self-sacrifice and radical generosity become increasing difficult options. In fact, studies show that (on average) the more people make, the less generous they become. Which is a major problem because Jesus calls us to be radical and generous—sometimes to the point of being reckless—and too often our wealth can become a major roadblock to God's calling on our lives.

In poker, sometimes you're up chips and sometimes you're down, but it is always easier to go "all in" and risk all your chips when you're down. If I only have a few chips and I get a good hand dealt to me, I hardly have to think twice before risking everything. But when I have a giant stack of chips that I worked hard to build over time, it becomes much harder, and feels much riskier, to go all in. Perhaps I am just a bad poker player, but when is it easiest for me to go "all in" in life? *When I have nothing to lose.* When my riches come from God alone. When you have much, it becomes difficult to risk it all, but that is exactly what Jesus wants us to do. He wants us to go all in and risk everything on what has been revealed to us.

Life is like playing a round of Texas hold 'em. You only get to see the two cards in your hand, and the vast majority of the cards are face down on the table, hidden away in the deck. You cannot see all the cards in poker, just as you cannot understand everything you would like to about the reality we live in. You cannot see all the cards, but you can see the Jesus card. There it is, sitting in your hand. You have a card that says "I am God, I became a man to reconcile you to me, and I love you completely." Sometimes that is just about all you get. The rest is hidden. And just like any round of poker, there is risk involved. In the face of our modern skepticism, cynicism, and personal doubts, are we willing to risk it?

God says to risk everything so that we can *taste* everything. To go "all in" so that we might drink even more deeply of the Kingdom of God. Jesus says that if we are willing to give up everything we will find something even better waiting for us.

Imagine that you were in the championship poker game in the middle of a crucial hand. As your opponent is aggressively raising the stakes, you somehow come to find out that you are going to win the hand. Imagine that you just *knew* it, deep down in your heart. You had a profound and definite feeling, deep down in your bones, that the next cards to be revealed would include that last ace you needed. Would you go all in? Would you honestly risk everything on that hand? Would you seize the moment in front of you, *risking* everything in order to *gain* everything? Or would you play it safe? Would you push out some of your chips, risking twenty percent of what you have? Or maybe thirty percent? And for what? In hopes that a better hand would be dealt the next time around?

God invites us to step out in faith, face the risk, and trust Him. He invites us to trust in what Jesus has given us, and to trust in what little we can see. That is why Jesus tells us not to be afraid of the people who threaten us, mock us, or look down on us for following Him, "*because everything that is hidden will be shown. Everything that is secret will be made known.*"[22] Trust that at the end of this life—at the end of the poker round—everything will be revealed to us. All the cards will be turned over, and no secrets will be left. Uncertainty will be cast out. In the end, everything will be unveiled and you will see what God has seen all along: that the game was fixed in His favor, that Jesus wins, and that love will triumph.

Right now we cannot see the other hands, and the vast majority of cards are facedown and hidden from us,

---

[22] Matthew 10:26.

so we have to trust that love will win. The gut-wrenching invitation from God is to go "all in" and embrace the risk by stepping into the adventure that He has for you.

Unfortunately, this is not what most of us want to hear. Most of us have spent our lives trying to avoid risk, not embrace it. We fear the unknown, we want guarantees, and we want insurance. We want safety, security, comfort, and healthy retirement accounts. But that is not how God operates. You cannot eliminate the element of risk involved in this game, nor should we obsess over trying.

I really wanted to break everything down and spell it out. I thought that if I could somehow make faith less of a risk, then more people might have faith. I thought maybe I could make everything feel logical and safe, but I can't. Not really. And when Jesus is walking on water, and invites us to step off the boat and walk on water with Him, we are not being called to choose safety, or even logic. I was educated as an attorney. We were trained to think as logically as possible, so it bothers me that the Gospel can feel so illogical. Sometimes it actually bothers me that Jesus' miracles and promises defy the typical human experience. If forces us to be governed by something other than logic, and to choose something beyond safety.

You want so badly to live in a logical world, but there you are, on a small wooden boat in the middle of a storm, and Jesus wants you to step out onto the water with Him. If you wanted to stay as safe as possible, you would have stayed on the shore. If you wanted to be as logical as possible, well . . . you would have to reject what is right in front of your eyes. But here you are, out on the boat, looking down at the rolling waves and wondering if you have gone mad. This is the human dilemma. We all stand on the edge of our own personal boats, grasping for something safe and logical, and wondering if we can actually trust the invitation to walk on water. And all the while there is this crazy love calling us.

We are caught in this paradoxical tension because the only place we are truly safe is in God's loving arms, but in order to get there we have to follow a call that looks totally unsafe (and illogical) in the eyes of the world. Everything in us fights to reject this, but we have to remind ourselves that God never promised that life would be safe and easy. He promised us that He is good. He tells us that He *is* love, and not a safe, logical, neat, tidy, controlled, restrained, or cautious love. God's love is wild and unrestrained. It is so completely different from what the world offers that it is difficult to describe, and I feel helpless as I grasp for words that do not satisfy. His love is counterintuitive and illogical and yet it is as real as anything I have ever known.

One of my favorite things in the world is a good sunset over the Pacific Ocean, but I doubt I will ever have the words to adequately describe one (let alone to someone who had never seen a sunset before). My words fall hopelessly short. In the same way, I doubt anyone can fit the labyrinth of God's love into words and onto paper. The only word I can use to describe it is *indescribable*, but I keep catching glimpses of it, and I know it to be real. It is more beautiful than the most superb and pristine beauty we can see in nature, or even the love we can experience with one another. It is an indescribable and illogical love that calls us. What choice do we have but to bet big?

I want so desperately to reduce God down to something predictable and safe, but I think I need to repent of that. If we could reduce God to something comfortable and safe,

He would not capture our hearts. Just as if you reduced the Pacific Ocean down to something tame and safe, you wouldn't feel a sense of awe when you stood at the edge of it. No one's heart was ever stirred while standing at the edge of a kiddie pool. We actually *need* something that is beyond our comprehension and control—something that requires courage and risk. Jesus is not calling us into what is known, easy, or simple. He is calling us to trust Him and step out even when we cannot explain everything, and even when we don't have all the answers.

Things are happening all around me that I cannot explain, things that force me to question the assumptions I keep trying to hold on to. God is speaking and moving. He is redeeming, healing, and restoring. He is really up to something in the world. In the midst of all of this, we cannot afford to cling to our old assumptions or claim science as our religion, anymore than we can afford to reject God and bathe in self-worship. We cannot afford to blind ourselves to the greater reality that is unfolding around us. Something exciting and mysterious is transpiring here that lies deeper than the gaze of science and beyond the reach of traditional logic.

Do I still have doubts? Sure I do! Do I understand it all? No way! Not yet. But I also have enough understanding to know I don't need to understand it all. I understand that paradox, tension, and uncertainty have a beauty to them, and that sometimes they are to be embraced (and even celebrated).

In the grand scheme of things, I will admit that I don't really know much. I cannot see all the cards and I do not have all the answers, *but I know the God who does.* I carry this crazy hope that one day everything will be revealed to us—that we'll be shown the deepest hidden truths about the reality we were living in, and any confusion or misguided assumptions we have carried up to that point will evaporate in the intensity of His glory. In the meantime, we bet big. We follow the impossible call of Jesus to walk on water, and we say yes to the life He has in store for us. We have the Jesus card, and a choice to make. Today we see dimly, and there is more at play than meets the eye, but I believe one day we will see clearly, and that will be a glorious day.

20 My Life in a Sentence

"Love the Lord your God with all your
heart and with all your soul and with all
your mind and with all your strength [and]
love your neighbor as yourself.
There is no commandment greater
than these."

– Jesus[23]

Back when I graduated from college, I lived in the
Greenlake neighborhood in Seattle. I was still pretty
young in my faith, and I was still trying to learn the
ropes and figure out what it meant to walk with Jesus,
but I was fortunate enough to figure out pretty early that
it's best done in community—shoulder to shoulder with
other people. So when my friend Jenna invited me to
her college group at church, I said yes. Not because I
was super excited to go, but because I knew I wasn't
supposed to follow Jesus alone, and sometimes we have
to do things because we know they will be good for us. Far
too often we let what is safe and comfortable trump what
is authentic and necessary. So I decided to go to church
with my friend. The service was better than I expected
(especially for being run by a college kid) and when the
sermon came to a close I turned and introduced myself to
the young man sitting behind me. He was an odd looking
kid with a kind demeanor. I told him my name was Matt
and he told me his name was Jackson. Then it came time
to start small talk. I was anticipating the typical questions
like *"how are you doing today?"* or *"do you live around*

---

[23]   Mark 12:30-31

here?" or "*how long have you been attending?*" These are the typical questions we ask strangers at church.

My immediate focus was actually on holding a good conversation without talking about our jobs. It was winter of 2008 and the economy had just crashed, so the last thing I wanted to do was ask the typical question "*what do you do?*" Half the 2008 graduates were unemployed, and no one wants to start small talk by telling a stranger how much time they spend on their mom's couch applying for jobs on Craigslist. We have this terrible habit of thinking that the job we work is what defines us, but there isn't much room for that in God's Kingdom. In turns out that pastors, carpenters, attorneys, and stay-at-home moms can all glorify God equally, and to be honest sometimes we just get stuck at a crappy job.

While I was busy trying to avoid the topic of employment, my new acquaintance opened up with the most difficult question I have ever had to answer. He simply told me his name, and then with a curious look on his face he asked, "*who are you?*" I was stunned by the question. He did not ask "*how are you?*" or "*who did you come with?*" or "*what do you do?*" I could have managed those, but instead he simply asked "*who are you?*" and I could tell by his tone he had not misspoken.

Normally quick on my feet, I was completely caught off guard as my mind began to race with scattered thoughts . . . *didn't I tell him my name already? Does he want to know what profession I'm in? Is he asking about my hobbies or what I do for fun?* No, I thought, none of those things are actually who I am. I am not my name, my hobbies, my pastimes, or even my personality. But how I could describe the essence of who I am to this stranger? My thoughts continued to race . . . *I don't even understand who I am or how to articulate it, much less in a single sentence!* I was stranded by the awkwardness of the question.

How could I describe the truest part of who I am (or even sum up what I believe) in a single sentence? At this point my thoughts were a panicked mess, as the seconds began ticking by (which felt like minutes) and my new friend sat and waited patiently for my answer. Apparently he was oblivious to my growing embarrassment. I considered saying something along the lines of "*someone who cares*" or maybe "*a nice guy trying to make a difference*" but it just sounded too sappy, and I knew there had to be a better answer.

By now the awkwardness was approaching a fever pitch and I was ready to end the misery, so I managed to squeak out the words . . . "*Um, I'm . . . I'm new here . . . and that is a good question.*" I know what you are thinking, profound response right? Fortunately, the conversation immediately flowed back into the realm of "normal" and I was relieved to answer everyday questions about where I worked and how long I had been part of the college group. But when the conversation died and the night finally ended, his original question resurfaced in my mind.

As I walked home that night I pondered it in my head. How could I have made it this far through life and still have no idea who I am? They don't teach you that in college. I am not my name. It is simply a word that was assigned to me when I was born. I am not my job because it will change. I am not my hobbies, habits, or accomplishments. I am not my personality because it changes as well. I am not even my physical body. The flesh and bones that everyone calls "Matt" have been constantly growing and developing. Its cells dying and replacing each other as I march through time. What is left of my two-year-old body, or my twenty-year-old body? All of those cells are dead and gone. My brain cells have been constantly handing off memories to the next generation by teaching them tales of the past, and my muscle cells have been diligently sharing their collective experiences with their willing replacements before going the way of all the earth. My old body is gone. But if I am not my cells, my hobbies, or my personality, then *who am I?*

Years have passed since I was first asked that question and I still do not have an adequate response, or at least not one that feels rich and satisfying. I cannot think of an answer that captures the essence and core of who I am. It is strange to come this far through life and still know so little about myself.

Ultimately I think the question is a difficult one because it is a matter of identity, and identity is complicated. Our identity can be built on our ethnicity, our possessions, our belief system, or even who we hang out with. We each choose (to varying degrees) what we place our identity in and how we will define ourselves. We engrave it on our own hearts and chart it into our life maps. We hold the pen that carves it, and somewhere deep down we have written: *"This is who I am."*

We play a central role in shaping our own identities, but the curious thing about identity is that it often seems to be a reflection of what we worship. We view ourselves in relation to the thing we value most in life. It is as if we were staring at the object of our worship while we penned our identity onto our hearts. The two are related. If we worship money, we will see ourselves in terms of rich and poor, and we will assign value to others based on their wealth. If we worship our careers then we will judge people based on what they do, and we will label ourselves a pilot, a teacher, or a drop out, and we think to ourselves, *"That's who I am."* If we worship alcohol we begin to see ourselves simply as the "party guy," and we begin to value others in relation to our lifestyle.

I think that is why God's first commandment to His redeemed people was to put Him first. I think that is why Jesus made it clear that the most important commandment is to love God with everything that we have. All our adoration, all our intellect, and all the strength we can muster. He wants us to worship God above everything else because the higher we hold God in our hearts and minds, the more He will influence our identities.

That is why I abandoned my streetlights and left my old life behind, so that I could love God with all my heart. I mean, not *all* my heart. I suppose if I loved God with my whole heart I would look more like Maximus, or Mother Teresa, or maybe even Jesus. I would be bold and fierce and full of life. If I could really die to myself, and trust completely in God, I might change the whole world. But to battle your whole heart and soul into submission is a crazy and lovely battle that never seems to end. It gets easier as it goes (and much more pleasant) but the process will never be complete this side of resurrection.

I still fall short of giving God everything, but I do love God, and I recognize that the burden is not on me to change the world (or even to change you) but rather I am supposed to start by simply accepting His love. Receiving God's love is the launch pad for loving God, and it makes no sense to attempt loving God before you have accepted His love. The reason I love God is not because I am some sort of saint. I love God because He first loved us. My love is a response; it is a reactionary love. When I was wandering, He came near. When I was in danger, He stepped in. When I was a slave to this world, He loved me enough to chase me down with reckless determination.

This idea really resonates with me: that God loves us (and loves His enemies) because we exist. He loves us because we are the center of His beautiful creation and He just has a heart to bless us. Each one of us is incredibly valuable in His eyes, so much so that His love does not fade when we turn our backs on Him, offend Him, deny Him, curse Him, and pound His limbs into a cross. He still just has this crazy love for us; the kind of love that melts hardened hearts and opens the eyes of the blind.

His type of love escapes words. I am a benefactor of it, I am a witness to it, but my words are weak. I have been stumbling after it long enough to have gained some insight, but I still feel completely overwhelmed when I try to articulate it. I grasp for words but come up empty. I have been rambling on for a whole book now and I am only scratching the surface.

I think this might be why God called himself the great "I AM." [24] There is no adjective that would be adequate to complete that sentence—nothing quite captures it. God says that from the beginning of time "I AM." *You are what, God? You are loving? Kind? Powerful?*

"*Sure,*" God responds, "*I am all of those things. But I am more than that. I am what I am, and always will*

---

[24] See Exodus 3:14.

be. I cannot be fully captured by any single word except 'indescribable,' and when you come close to me, and I reveal myself to you, you'll know that it's true." That is the God who pursues us. What a beautiful world we live in.

I believe relationships are the most important thing in life, and our most important relationship is the one we have with God. If we have a healthy biblical relationship with Jesus then all our other relationships will be transformed. Our relationship with money, our friends, our spouse, and the planet all begin to change; life gets breathed into dark corners, light floods in and overwhelms death. God makes us into new creations that respect all of creation, that forgive because we are forgiven, and love our friends, our spouses, and even our enemies because we are filled with a radical love. We need only to accept the invitation in order for this transformation to begin.

In a broad sense the purpose of life is to glorify God, and I typically think this means *doing* something, but the most important element of our purpose is actually *being.* Our purpose is to be loved by God. The ultimate goal is actually very simple: accept God's love. Being loved is simpler and even more profound than seeking to glorify God through our actions, because being loved is not about doing, performing, or accomplishing. It is simply about being. Just be. Simply exist in the state God created you to experience. The state of being loved unconditionally and unceasingly. The rest will work itself out. As we learn to walk in the Spirit, we naturally begin to live in His life-giving rhythms.

Filled with the love of God's Spirit, we do not need to be constantly told what to do or say. We do not require constant encouragement (or chastising) in order do the right things. We tend to just do them. The greater capacity we have to accept God's love, the easier it is to love others. This becomes even more true the longer we walk, and the closer we draw to God's Spirit. Divine love can become a way of life if we let it. The very process of chasing after this love changes us, transforms us, and redeems us, and the Bible says that as we are redeemed *God* is glorified. It is all for His glory.

Consider the alternative: without this love, we cannot truly glorify God at all. Without the Spirit of Love leading us, we *cannot* please God. The more we try on our own, the more we typically commit misguided and even harmful acts in His name. Accepting this love is a struggle, but it is essential to our walk. The most important thing about you (whether you realize it or not) is that you are deeply loved by your Creator.

So when forced to answer the question *"who are you?"* the best answer I can give is this: *"a human being, who is loved by God."* That is the core and unchanging essence of who I am. I am a unique cluster of DNA, body cells, and a soul set adrift on a planet in a potentially infinite universe who sometimes feels sinful, alone, and inadequate, but who is nonetheless slowly learning to trust in a magnificent yet unseen God—a God who is slowly but surely transforming this broken heart. And if I am crazy (which is possible) I hope I am crazy in all the right ways.

21 Still Speaking

A brisk breeze sends shivers down my spine as the moonlight dances off wintery Lake Washington. My friends and family have all gone to bed or retired to the couch for late-night television, but not me. I snuck off to the dock on this crisp winter night to seek God. Most of my generation thinks that God stopped talking a long time ago (if He ever started talking to begin with) but the longer I live, the more I question those assumptions. I think we live in a God-soaked universe and we just need eyes to see it. As the waves roll under the dock and lap against the shore, I stare up at a full moon and wonder what it means to live a life that is full and rich; a life that has substance and weight. I wonder what it would look like to be an agent of light. I want to live a life that has meaning and significance. I want to taste the fullness of it and be blown away by its beauty. Looking back toward the house, I can see the silhouettes of the people I love through the windows, outlined by the glow of florescent rays as they dance along the walls and ceilings.

We don't have a functioning TV at my house, and it can be hard for a guy in his twenties to go without a TV. Most eight-year-olds are more in touch with foreign affairs and who is pregnant in Hollywood, but the disconnect is worth it. I am craving something more than cathode rays and pop culture. My heart starves for a truth deeper than what CNN has to offer. That is why I have come to sit on the dock by Lake Washington in late December, to watch the moon dance in and out of thick clouds as frost begins to form on the ground. I want to know what it means to be truly alive. I want to live with my eyes wide open, and be connected with Love in this moment that graces me. I want to live with an awareness of God's presence and seize the life He offers. I refuse to let another day slip by where I feel half-asleep.

I don't think God is done talking to us. In fact, I don't think He ever stopped. I wonder out loud what it is God wants to say to our generation. I wonder what He would have us do. I wonder how we might go about finding abundant life in a sea of mediocrity and half-truths.

I think God wants us to understand that He is with us and He is bigger than our problems. I think He wants to encourage us in the fact that evil will not endure forever, but that one day He will put an end to it. He wants us to live in light of the fact that one day heaven and earth will collide. As I ponder these things the clouds break, revealing the stars in all their beauty, and hundreds of little lights shine down through a crisp winter sky. All at once, my mind runs wild thinking about how big and endless the universe is and how there is no such thing as up and down because the world is round and the universe stretches out in every direction and we can't find the edges.

This is why I don't watch TV. My mind can hardly stay focused as it is. I don't need help encouraging my hyperactive thoughts. Most of the time I cannot sit still and listen long enough to hear what God might be saying. Most of us cannot stay off our iPhones long enough to tune in, but God is still speaking. I think He wants to tell us that His way is better, and that His way is best when we walk it with Him.

Perhaps it is up there, written into that vast array of stars. For if those stars were forged by a hand, that hand would know no limits. Any purposes He created would be known fully by Him alone. His power would be limited only by His own nature—the nature of love—and the self-limits imposed by love. He would have the capacity to command the wind and the waves; the forces of nature would yield and bow. Parting the Red Sea would be nothing. Turning the material make-up of water into wine would be perfectly conceivable, because He would be in, above, over, and through that vast swirling universe of galaxies. His Kingdom would be an unstoppable force, and He would be worth following at any cost.

I think God is a dreamer. I think He has a vision for this reality, something that is achievable right here and now. I think He is looking for friends who will just say yes, and not criticize or analyze or give their top ten best excuses. He wants people who catch wind of the vision, who see the beauty in it, and who want to come along for the adventure—even if the invitation sounds like a four hundred mile bike ride and you don't own a bike yet.

I think life was meant to be quite a bit simpler than we have made it out to be. We were meant to have less stuff and more beauty, more kindness and less complication. Know God, love your neighbor as yourself, and don't worry so much. Don't worry about stuff or sin or coming in last or dying. So much of life's beauty is in the simple things, and if we pave over them trying to create a superhighway to our material and social ends, we won't have much left to enjoy when we get there. Find the things you can rely on in this life, and rely on them. Find the things you can learn from, and learn from them. Find the things you wish to become—the things you were meant to be—and do your best to become them. Life is too short to struggle through it blindly by wasting our time chasing things we do not need, hating people that ought to be forgiven, or trying to impress people that really are not worth impressing.

Know yourself and be true to yourself. Know God and be true to God. Lean into redemption and live for the renewal of all things. The rest will work itself out. This whole messy life is ours for just a moment. It is just a flash of energy, tension, and love before we are gone.

In the meantime we find ourselves here beneath the streetlights. Blinded, confused, and overwhelmed, but never abandoned. Begging to be rescued, but never alone. Catching glimpses of the Kingdom, but starving for what is yet to come. Flooded with doubts, but awakening to the fact that there is something more going on than meets the eye.

Amid all the chaos, controversy, labeling, religion, and questioning, there stands something unchanging and unwavering. His love is relentless, unswerving, and unfailing. His hands crafted the stars of our distant universe, and were pierced by the nails of a roman soldier. His hands knit you together in the womb, and they were stretched out on a cross so that Light could conquer death. His hands long to carry you home. They long to carry you away from hopelessness, loneliness, and hell itself. Away from streetlights, self-addiction, sin, and stress. They long to carry you through death and into eternity. Our job is simple: wake up to that reality . . . and react.

With love,

-Matt

mattdeisen@gmail.com

"And surely I am with you always, to the very end of the age . . ."

– Jesus[25]

Special thanks to Christine Swanson for the illustrations, and to Jake and Kate Hiester, Matt O'Brien, Sophie Ferguson, Caitie Poland, Brandon Perkins, Evan Wickham, and my wife Abigail. Without your support this book would never have been published.

About the Author

Educated as an attorney and raised in an atheist home, Matt Deisen came to faith in Jesus while attending college in Seattle. Matt, his wife Abigail, and their infant son recently moved from Portland, Oregon to Spokane, Washington to plant a church.